READING COMPREHENSION
SUCCESS

IN 20 MINUTES A DAY

Elizabeth Chesla

LearningExpress

New York

Updated and revised in 2002.

Library of Congress Cataloging-in-Publication Data

Chesla, Elizabeth L.

 Reading comprehension success in 20 minutes a day/Elizabeth Chesla.

  p. cm.—(Skill builders series)

 ISBN 1–57685–126–5

  1. Reading comprehension—Problems, exercises, etc. I. Title.

 II. Series: Skilll builders series (New York, N.Y.)

LB1050.45.C45 1998

428.4—dc21   98–12958

                       CIP

Printed in the United States of America

19 18 17 16 15 14 13

Second Edition

For Further Information

For information on LearningExpress, other LearningExpress products, or bulk sales, please call or write to us at:

 LearningExpress™

 900 Broadway

 Suite 604

 New York, NY 10003

 212-995-2566

Or visit us at:

 www.learnatest.com

An Important Note to
Our Library Readers

LEARNINGEXPRESS
Skill Builders Series

Introducing a new series that helps build basic skills *fast*. Each book offers essential tips and techniques plus plenty of practice exercises in critical skill areas. Ideal for individuals preparing to take a basic skills exam. A must for those who need to polish the skills that lead to success.

Practical Math Success in 20 Minutes a Day
Reading Comprehension Success in 20 Minutes a Day
Reasoning Skills Success in 20 Minutes a Day
Vocabulary & Spelling Success in 20 Minutes a Day
Writing Skills Success in 20 Minutes a Day

All LearningExpress books are available at your local bookstore, or call us toll free at 888-551-JOBS.

If You're Taking a Job Entrance or National Standards Exam . . .

You've come to the right place! The 20 lessons in this book are designed to help you prepare for the reading comprehension section of your exam. You'll move from short passages and easy questions to longer, more complex passages and harder questions, learning how to answer all kinds of questions you might be asked as you work through the lessons. Examples and practice exercises are presented in test format and will give you plenty of practice. So come exam day . . . you'll be prepared to score your best.

CONTENTS

Language and Style

Reading Between the Lines

HOW TO USE
THIS BOOK

This book is designed to help you improve your reading comprehension skills by studying 20 minutes a day for 20 days. You'll start with the basics and move into more complex reading comprehension and critical thinking strategies. Please note that although each chapter can be an effective skill builder on its own, it is important that you proceed through this book in order, from Lesson 1 through Lesson 20. Each lesson builds on skills and ideas discussed in the previous chapters. As you move through this book and your reading skills develop, the passages you read will increase both in length and in complexity.

The book begins with a pretest, which will allow you to see how well you can answer various kinds of reading comprehension question *now*, as you start out. When you finish the book, take the post-test to see how much you've improved.

The text is divided into four sections, each focusing on a different group of related reading and thinking strategies. These strategies will be outlined at the beginning of each section and then reviewed in a special "putting it all together" final lesson.

Each lesson provides several exercises that allow you to practice the skills you learn. To help you be sure you're on the right track, each lesson also provides answers and explanations for all of the practice questions. You will also find practical suggestions in each chapter for how to continue practicing these skills throughout the rest of the day and the week.

The most important thing you can do to improve your reading skills is to become an active reader. Really, this whole book is about becoming an active reader. But the rest of this introduction will tell you a few of the most important points about active reading, so you can start practicing them right away in Lesson 1.

BECOMING AN ACTIVE READER

Critical reading and thinking skills require active reading. Being an active reader means you have to engage yourself with the text, both mentally and physically. Active readers generally do this in three ways:

- By skimming ahead and jumping back
- By marking up the text
- By making specific observations about the text

SKIMMING AHEAD AND JUMPING BACK

Skimming ahead enables you to see what's coming up in your reading. Page through the text you're about to read. Notice how the text is broken down, what the main topics are, and the order in which they are covered. Notice key words and ideas that are boldfaced, bulleted, boxed, or otherwise highlighted. By skimming through the text like this beforehand, you prepare yourself for your reading task. It's a lot like checking out the hills and curves in the course before a cross-country race. If you know what's ahead, you know how to pace yourself, and you're prepared to handle what's to come.

When you finish your reading task, jump back. Review the summaries, headings, and highlighted information in the text. Include both what the author highlighted and what you highlighted. By jumping back, you help to solidify in your mind the ideas and information you just read. You're reminded of how each idea fits into the whole, how ideas and information are connected. When you make connections between ideas, you're much more likely to remember them.

MARKING UP THE TEXT

Marking up the text creates a direct physical link between you and the words you're reading. It forces you to pay closer attention to the words that you read and takes you to a higher level of comprehension. Marking up the text includes three specific strategies:

- Highlighting or underlining key words and ideas
- Circling and defining any unfamiliar words or phrases
- Recording your reactions and questions in the margins

Highlighting or Underlining Key Ideas

When you highlight or underline key words and ideas, you mark the most important parts of the text you are reading. There's an important skill at work here: You can't highlight or underline everything, so you have to distinguish between the facts and ideas that are most important (major ideas) and those facts and ideas that are helpful but not so important (minor or supporting ideas). You want to highlight only the major ideas, so you don't end up with a text that's completely highlighted.

When your text is highlighted, you'll benefit much more from a review of the text—when you jump back, you'll be quickly reminded of the most important ideas to remember. Having highlighted or underlined major ideas also helps you remember more clearly what you've read.

Circling Unfamiliar Words

One of the most important habits to develop is that of circling and looking up unfamiliar words and phrases. If possible, don't sit down to read without a dictionary by your side. It is not uncommon for the meaning of an entire sentence to hinge on the meaning of a single word or phrase, and if you don't know what that word or phrase means, you won't understand the sentence. Besides, this habit enables you to quickly and steadily expand your vocabulary, and you'll be a more confident reader and speaker as a result.

If you don't have a dictionary readily available, try to determine the meaning of the word as best you can from its context—that is, the words and ideas around it. (There's more on this topic in Lesson 3.) Then, make sure you look up the word as soon as possible so you're sure what it means.

Making Marginal Notes

Recording your questions and reactions in the margins turns you from a passive receiver of information into an active participant in a dialogue. (If you're reading a library book, write your reactions in a notebook.) You will get much more out of the ideas and information you read about if you create a "conversation" with the writer. Here are some examples of the kinds of reactions you might write down in the margin or in your notebook:

- **Questions** often come up when you read. They may be answered later in the text, but by that time you may have forgotten the question! And if your question isn't answered, you may want to bring it up with a friend or former teacher: "Why does the writer describe the new welfare policy as 'unfair'?" or "Why does the character react in this way?"

- **Agreements and disagreements** with the author are bound to come up if you're reading actively. Write them down: "That's not necessarily true!" or "This policy makes a lot of sense to me."

- **Connections** you note can be either between the text and something that you read earlier or between the text and your own experience. For example, "I remember feeling the same way when I . . . ." or "This is similar to what happened in China."

- **Evaluations** are your way of keeping the author honest. If you think the author isn't providing sufficient support for what he or she is saying, or that there's something wrong with that support, say so: "He says the dropping of the bomb was inevitable, but he doesn't explain why" or "This is a very selfish reason."

MAKING OBSERVATIONS

Good readers know that writers use many different strategies to express their ideas. Even if you know very little about those strategies, you can make useful observations about what you read that will help you better understand and remember the author's ideas. You can notice, for example, the author's choice of words; the structure of the sentences and paragraphs; any repetition of words or ideas; important details about people, places, and things; and so on.

This step—making observations—is essential because your observations, what you notice, are what lead you to logical inferences about what you read. *Inferences* are conclusions based on reason, fact, or evidence. You are constantly making inferences based on your observations, even when you're not reading. For example, if you notice that the sky is full of dark, heavy clouds, you might infer that it is going to rain; if you notice that your co-worker has a stack of gardening books on her desk, you might infer that she likes gardening.

If you misunderstand what you read, it is often because you haven't looked closely enough at the text. As a result, you base your inferences on your own ideas and experiences, not on what's actually written in the text. You end up forcing your own ideas on the author rather than listening to what the author has to say and then forming your own ideas about it. It's critical, then, that you begin to really pay attention to what writers say and how they say it.

If any of this sounds a bit confusing now, don't worry. Each of these ideas will be explained thoroughly in the lessons that follow. What's important in the meantime is that you start practicing active reading as best you can. Begin by taking the pretest.

PRETEST

Before you start your study of reading skills, you may want to get an idea of how much you already know and how much you need to learn. If that's the case, take the pretest that follows. The pretest is 50 multiple-choice questions covering all the lessons in this book. Naturally, 50 questions can't cover every single concept or strategy you will learn by working through this book. So even if you get all of the questions on the pretest right, it's almost guaranteed that you will find a few ideas or reading tactics in this book that you didn't already know. On the other hand, if you get a lot of the answers wrong on this pretest, don't despair. This book will show you how to read more effectively, step by step.

So use this pretest just to get a general idea of how much of what's in this book you already know. If you get a high score on this pretest, you may be able to spend less time with this book than you originally planned. If you get a low score, you may find that you will need more than 20 minutes a day to get through each chapter and improve your reading skills.

There's an answer sheet you can use for filling in the correct answers on the next page. Or, if you prefer, simply circle the answer numbers in this book. If the book doesn't belong to you, write the numbers 1–50 on a piece of paper and record your answers there. Take as much time as you need to do this short test. When you finish, check your answers against the answer key at the end of this lesson. Each answer tells you which lesson of this book teaches you about the reading strategy in that question.

1.	ⓐ	ⓑ	ⓒ	ⓓ	21.	ⓐ	ⓑ	ⓒ	ⓓ	41.	ⓐ	ⓑ	ⓒ	ⓓ
2.	ⓐ	ⓑ	ⓒ	ⓓ	22.	ⓐ	ⓑ	ⓒ	ⓓ	42.	ⓐ	ⓑ	ⓒ	ⓓ
3.	ⓐ	ⓑ	ⓒ	ⓓ	23.	ⓐ	ⓑ	ⓒ	ⓓ	43.	ⓐ	ⓑ	ⓒ	ⓓ
4.	ⓐ	ⓑ	ⓒ	ⓓ	24.	ⓐ	ⓑ	ⓒ	ⓓ	44.	ⓐ	ⓑ	ⓒ	ⓓ
5.	ⓐ	ⓑ	ⓒ	ⓓ	25.	ⓐ	ⓑ	ⓒ	ⓓ	45.	ⓐ	ⓑ	ⓒ	ⓓ
6.	ⓐ	ⓑ	ⓒ	ⓓ	26.	ⓐ	ⓑ	ⓒ	ⓓ	46.	ⓐ	ⓑ	ⓒ	ⓓ
7.	ⓐ	ⓑ	ⓒ	ⓓ	27.	ⓐ	ⓑ	ⓒ	ⓓ	47.	ⓐ	ⓑ	ⓒ	ⓓ
8.	ⓐ	ⓑ	ⓒ	ⓓ	28.	ⓐ	ⓑ	ⓒ	ⓓ	48.	ⓐ	ⓑ	ⓒ	ⓓ
9.	ⓐ	ⓑ	ⓒ	ⓓ	29.	ⓐ	ⓑ	ⓒ	ⓓ	49.	ⓐ	ⓑ	ⓒ	ⓓ
10.	ⓐ	ⓑ	ⓒ	ⓓ	30.	ⓐ	ⓑ	ⓒ	ⓓ	50.	ⓐ	ⓑ	ⓒ	ⓓ
11.	ⓐ	ⓑ	ⓒ	ⓓ	31.	ⓐ	ⓑ	ⓒ	ⓓ					
12.	ⓐ	ⓑ	ⓒ	ⓓ	32.	ⓐ	ⓑ	ⓒ	ⓓ					
13.	ⓐ	ⓑ	ⓒ	ⓓ	33.	ⓐ	ⓑ	ⓒ	ⓓ					
14.	ⓐ	ⓑ	ⓒ	ⓓ	34.	ⓐ	ⓑ	ⓒ	ⓓ					
15.	ⓐ	ⓑ	ⓒ	ⓓ	35.	ⓐ	ⓑ	ⓒ	ⓓ					
16.	ⓐ	ⓑ	ⓒ	ⓓ	36.	ⓐ	ⓑ	ⓒ	ⓓ					
17.	ⓐ	ⓑ	ⓒ	ⓓ	37.	ⓐ	ⓑ	ⓒ	ⓓ					
18.	ⓐ	ⓑ	ⓒ	ⓓ	38.	ⓐ	ⓑ	ⓒ	ⓓ					
19.	ⓐ	ⓑ	ⓒ	ⓓ	39.	ⓐ	ⓑ	ⓒ	ⓓ					
20.	ⓐ	ⓑ	ⓒ	ⓓ	40.	ⓐ	ⓑ	ⓒ	ⓓ					

PRETEST

The pretest consists of a series of reading passages with questions that follow to test your comprehension.

Mt. Kindred Adds Psychology Courses

Mount Kindred College hopes to draw more students from the community with two new early childhood course offerings this fall. Department Chair Jane Fairbanks announced Tuesday that the course titles will be The Myth of the Difficult Child and Three R's or Two T's?: Real Learning or Tantrums in Tandem? The latter course will be an observational lab held at The Learning Academy, the preschool on campus.

New faculty member Dr. Allison Landers will instruct both courses. Landers received her Ph.D. in 1995 from Northwestern University, where she wrote a dissertation on the pedagogical effectiveness of preschools. According to Fairbanks, Dr. Landers concluded that academic results are questionable, but that preschools have extensive side benefits.

The courses are part of Mount Kindred's Project Outreach, which aims to draw more non-traditional students to the college. The project was initiated in 1993, according to Dr. Fairbanks, in order to better serve the five-county area. Mount Kindred is the only college in the region, and the governor-appointed Board of Trustees mandated that more efforts be made to involve the community in college programs. Dr. Fairbanks also disclosed that the college's enrollment has fallen ten percent over the past five years, while the state university in Unionville has seen an increase in enrollment.

The observational course meets one of the Psychology bachelor program lab requirements. It may also be of special interest to parents who wish a greater understanding of childhood learning behaviors. The Myth of the Difficult Child is scheduled on weekday evenings in order to make it easier for working parents to attend. Contact the Psychology Department at 777-4531 for more information, or drop by the office in Powell Hall. Other college departments will be announcing Project Outreach courses in the coming weeks. For a complete listing, refer to the fall course catalogue, available at the Crabtree, the campus bookstore, beginning August 1.

1. The Myth of the Difficult Child course will be held
   a. in Unionville, in order to attract students attending the university there
   b. at the campus pre-school, to allow direct observation of learning environments
   c. at night, for the convenience of people who work during the daytime
   d. in the early morning, so working parents can trade off child-care responsibilities

2. Which of the following statements is correct?
   a. Professor Landers will teach both courses.
   b. People wanting course catalogues should call the Psychology Department.
   c. The new courses begin August 1.
   d. The campus pre-school is called the Crabtree.

3. According to Jane Fairbanks, what was the direct cause of Project Outreach?
a. The Psychology faculty believed that members of the community should develop a greater understanding of their children's education.
b. Professor Lander's talents and interests were particularly suited to community involvement.
c. The Board of Trustees was appointed by the governor in 1993 and needed to find ways to spend its budget.
d. The Board of Trustees directed Mount Kindred College to strengthen its community involvement efforts.

4. Which of the following factors is implied as another reason for Project Outreach?
a. Enrollment has been going down, and the college wishes to attract more students.
b. The college has discriminated against lower-income community members in the past.
c. Many parents who have previously studied psychology live in the five-county area.
d. The Board of Trustees wants a more academically vigorous curriculum.

5. From the context of the passage, it can be determined that the word "pedagogical" in Professor Lander's dissertation is related to
a. unfair attitudes
b. teaching
c. psychological disorders
d. behavior

6. The "Myth of the Difficult Child" course title implies that Professor Landers
a. believes that telling stories about children will help us understand them better
b. wants to convince her students of the need for strong behavior controls
c. questions the validity of the label "difficult" when applied to children
d. thinks poorly behaved children tell stories in order to justify their behavior

7. Which of the following correctly states the primary subject of this news article?
a. the politics guiding the decision of the Board of Trustees that led to the establishment of Project Outreach
b. Professor Lander's appointment to Mount Kindred College's Psychology Department
c. two new early childhood psychology course offerings at Mount Kindred College
d. the needs of the community in relation to Mount Kindred College

8. This article is organized in which of the following ways?
a. in chronological order, from the past to the future
b. most important information first, followed by background and details
c. background first, followed by the most important information and details
d. as sensational news, with the most controversial topic first

(excerpt from the opening of an untitled essay)

John Steinbeck's *Grapes of Wrath*, published in 1939, was followed ten years later by A. B. Guthrie's *The Way West*. Both books chronicle a migration, though that of Guthrie's pioneers is considerably less bleak in origin. What strikes one at first glance, however, are the commonalties. Both Steinbeck's and Guthrie's characters are primarily farmers. They look to their destinations with nearly religious enthusiasm, imagining their "promised" land the way the Biblical Israelites envisioned Canaan. Both undergo great hardship to make the trek. But the two sagas differ distinctly in origin. Steinbeck's Oklahomans are forced off their land by the banks who own their mortgages, and they follow a false promise—that jobs await them as seasonal laborers in California. Guthrie's farmers willingly remove themselves, selling their land and trading their old dreams for their new hope in Oregon. The pioneers' decision to leave their farms in Missouri and the East is frivolous and ill-founded in comparison with the Oklahomans' unwilling response to displacement. Yet it is they, the pioneers, whom our history books declare the heroes.

9. From the context of the passage, it can be determined that the word "frivolous" most nearly means
   a. silly
   b. high-minded
   c. difficult
   d. calculated

10. Suppose that the author is considering following this sentence with supportive detail: "Both undergo great hardship to make the trek." Which of the following sentences would be in keeping with the comparison and contrast structure of the paragraph?
   a. The migrants in *The Way West* cross the Missouri, then the Kaw, and make their way overland to the Platte.
   b. The Oklahomans' jalopies break down repeatedly, while the pioneers' wagons need frequent repairs.
   c. Today's travelers would consider it a hardship to spend several days, let alone several months, getting anywhere.
   d. The Joad family, in *The Grapes of Wrath*, loses both grandmother and grandfather before the journey is complete.

11. Which of the following excerpts from the essay is an opinion, rather than a fact?
   a. "Both Steinbeck's and Guthrie's characters are primarily farmers."
   b. "Steinbeck's Oklahomans are forced off their land by the banks who own their mortgages…."
   c. "John Steinbeck's *Grapes of Wrath*, published in 1939, was followed ten years later by A. B. Guthrie's *The Way West*."
   d. "The pioneers' decision to leave their farms in Missouri and the East is frivolous and ill-founded in comparison with the Oklahomans'…."

12. The language in the paragraph implies that which of the following will happen to the Oklahomans when they arrive in California?
   a. They will find a means to practice their religion freely.
   b. They will be declared national heroes.
   c. They will not find the jobs they hoped for.
   d. They will make their livings as mechanics rather than as farm laborers.

Bill Clinton's Inaugural Address
(excerpt from the opening)

When George Washington first took the oath I have just sworn to uphold, news traveled slowly across the land by horseback, and across the ocean by boat. Now the sights and sounds of this ceremony are broadcast instantaneously to billions around the world. Communications and commerce are global. Investment is mobile. Technology is almost magical, and ambition for a better life is now universal.

We earn our livelihood in America today in peaceful competition with people all across the Earth. Profound and powerful forces are shaking and remaking our world, and the urgent question of our time is whether we can make change our friend and not our enemy. This new world has already enriched the lives of millions of Americans who are able to compete and win in it. But when most people are working harder for less; when others cannot work at all; when the cost of health care devastates families and threatens to bankrupt our enterprises, great and small; when the fear of crime robs law-abiding citizens of their freedom; and when millions of poor children cannot even imagine the lives we are calling them to lead, we have not made change our friend.

13. What is the central topic of the speech so far?
    a. how Americans can keep up with global competition
    b. ways in which technology has undermined our economy
    c. ways in which technology has improved our lives
    d. how change has affected America and our need to adapt

14. By comparing our times with those of George Washington, Bill Clinton demonstrates
    a. how apparently different, but actually similar, the two eras are
    b. how drastically technology has speeded up communications
    c. that presidential inaugurations receive huge media attention
    d. that television is a much more convincing communications tool than print

15. When President Clinton says that "most people are working harder for less," he is
    a. reaching a reasonable conclusion based on evidence he has provided
    b. reaching an unreasonable conclusion based on evidence he has provided
    c. making a generalization that would require evidence before it could be confirmed
    d. making a generalization that is so obvious that evidence is not needed

16. Assuming that Clinton wants to add something about crime being a more serious threat in our time than in George Washington's, which of the following sentences would be most consistent with the tone of the presidential speech?
    a. If I'd been alive in George's day, I would have enjoyed knowing that my wife and child could walk city streets without being mugged.
    b. In George Washington's time, Americans may not have enjoyed as many luxuries, but they could rest in the awareness that their neighborhoods were safe.
    c. George could at least count on one thing. He knew that his family was safe from crime.
    d. A statistical analysis of the overall growth in crime rates since 1789 would reveal that a significant increase has taken place.

The Crossing
Chapter I: The Blue Wall
(excerpt from the opening of a novel by Winston Churchill)

I was born under the Blue Ridge, and under that side which is blue in the evening light, in a wild land of game and forest and rushing waters. There, on the borders of a creek that runs into the Yadkin River, in a cabin that was chinked with red mud, I came into the world a subject of King George the Third, in that part of his realm known as the province of North Carolina.

The cabin reeked of corn-pone and bacon, and the odor of pelts. It had two shakedowns, on one of which I slept under a bearskin. A rough stone chimney was reared outside, and the fireplace was as long as my father was tall. There was a crane in it, and a bake kettle; and over it great buckhorns held my father's rifle when it was not in use. On other horns hung jerked bear's meat and venison hams, and gourds for drinking cups, and bags of seed, and my father's best hunting shirt; also, in a neglected corner, several articles of woman's attire from pegs. These once belonged to my mother. Among them was a gown of silk, of a fine, faded pattern, over which I was wont to speculate. The women at the Cross-Roads, twelve miles away, were dressed in coarse butternut wool and huge sunbonnets. But when I questioned my father on these matters he would give me no answers.

My father was—how shall I say what he was? To this day I can only surmise many things of him. He was a Scotchman born, and I know now that he had a slight Scotch accent. At the time of which I write, my early childhood, he was a frontiersman and hunter. I can see him now, with his hunting shirt and leggins and moccasins; his powder horn, engraved with wondrous scenes; his bullet pouch and tomahawk and hunting knife. He was a tall, lean man with a strange, sad face. And he talked little save when he drank too many "horns," as they were called in that country. These lapses of my father's were a perpetual source of wonder to me—and, I must say, of delight. They occurred only when a passing traveler who hit his fancy chanced that way, or, what was almost as rare, a neighbor. Many a winter night I have lain awake under the skins, listening to a flow of language that held me spellbound, though I understood scarce a word of it.

"Virtuous and vicious every man must be,

Few in the extreme, but all in a degree."

The chance neighbor or traveler was no less struck with wonder. And many the time have I heard the query, at the Cross-Roads and elsewhere, "Whar Alec Trimble got his larnin'?"

17. Why did the narrator enjoy it when his father drank too many "horns," or drafts of liquor?

   a. The father spoke brilliantly at those times.

   b. The boy was then allowed to do as he pleased.

   c. These were the only times when the father was not abusive.

   d. The boy was allowed to sample the drink himself.

18. Judging by the sentences surrounding it, the word "surmise" in the third paragraph most nearly means

   a. to form a negative opinion

   b. to praise

   c. to desire

   d. to guess

19. The mention of the dress in the second paragraph is most likely meant to

   a. show the similarity between its owner and other members of the community

   b. show how warm the climate was

   c. show the dissimilarity between its owner and other members of the community

   d. give us insight into the way most of the women of the region dressed

20. It can be inferred from the passage that Alec Trimble is

   a. a traveler

   b. a neighbor

   c. the narrator's father

   d. a poet

21. What is the meaning of the lines of verse quoted in the passage?

   a. Men who pretend to be virtuous are actually vicious.

   b. Moderate amounts of virtuousness and viciousness are present in all men.

   c. Virtuous men cannot also be vicious.

   d. Whether men are virtuous or vicious depends on the difficulty of their circumstances.

22. Which of the following adjectives best describes the region in which the cabin is located?

   a. remote

   b. urban

   c. agricultural

   d. flat

23. The author most likely uses dialect when quoting the question "Whar Alec Trimble got his larnin'?" in order to

   a. show disapproval of the father's drinking

   b. show how people talked down to the narrator

   c. show the speakers' lack of education

   d. mimic the way the father talked

(excerpt from a letter to a pet sitter)

Dear Lee,

   As I told you, I'll be gone until Wednesday morning. Thank you so much for taking on my "children" while I'm away. Like real children, they can be kind of irritating sometimes, but I'm going to enjoy myself so much more knowing they're getting some kind human attention. Remember that Regina (the "queen" in Latin, and she acts like one) is teething. If you don't watch her, she'll chew anything, including her sister, the cat. There are plenty of chew toys around the house. Whenever she starts gnawing on anything illegal, just divert her with one of those. She generally settles right down to a good hour-long chew. Then you'll see her wandering around whimpering with the remains of the toy in her mouth. She gets really frustrated because what she wants is to bury the thing. She'll try to dig a hole between the cushions of the couch. Finding that unsatisfactory, she'll wander some more, discontent, until you solve her problem for her. I usually show her the laundry basket, moving a few clothes so she can bury her toy beneath them. I do sound like a parent, don't I? You have to understand, my own son is practically grown up.

   Regina's food is the Puppy Chow in the utility room, where the other pet food is kept. Give her a bowl once in the morning and once in the evening. No more than that, no matter how much she begs. Beagles are notorious over-eaters, according to her breeder, and I don't want her to lose her girlish figure. She can share Rex (the King's) water, but be sure it's changed daily. She needs to go out several times a day, especially last thing at night and first thing in the morning. Let her stay out for about ten minutes each time, so she can do *all* her business. She also needs a walk in the afternoon, after which it's important to romp with her for awhile in the yard. The game she loves most is fetch, but be sure to make her drop the ball. She'd rather play tug of war with it. Tell her, "Sit!" Then when she does, say, "Drop it!" Be sure to tell her "good girl," and then throw the ball for her. I hope you'll enjoy these sessions as much as I do.

   Now, for the other two, Rex and Paws… (*letter continues*)

24. The tone of this letter is best described as
   a. chatty and humorous
   b. logical and precise
   c. confident and trusting
   d. condescending and preachy

25. If the pet sitter is a business-like professional who watches people's pets for a living, she or he would likely prefer
   a. more first-person revelations about the owner
   b. fewer first-person revelations about the owner
   c. more praise for agreeing to watch the animals
   d. greater detail on the animals' cute behavior

26. According to the author, his or her attachment to the pets derives at least partially from
   a. their regal pedigrees and royal bearing
   b. having few friends to pass the time with
   c. these particular animals' exceptional needs
   d. a desire to continue parenting

27. The information in the note is sufficient to determine that there are three animals. They are
   a. two cats and a dog
   b. three dogs
   c. a dog, a cat, and an unspecified animal
   d. a cat, a dog, and a parrot

28. Given that there are three animals to feed, which of the following arrangements of the feeding instructions would be most efficient and easiest to follow?

a. all given in one list, chronologically from morning to night

b. provided separately as they are for Regina, within separate passages on each animal

c. given in the order of quantities needed, the most to the least.

d. placed in the middle of the letter, where they would be least likely to be overlooked.

29. From the context of the note, it is most likely that the name "Rex" comes from the

a. Spanish language

b. English language

c. French language

d. Latin language

30. If the sitter is to follow the owner's directions in playing fetch with Regina, at what point will he or she will tell Regina "good girl"?

a. every time Regina goes after the ball

b. after Regina finds the ball

c. when Regina brings the ball back

d. after Regina drops the ball

(excerpt from an anti-hunting essay)

The practice of hunting is barbaric and shouldn't be allowed within the national forests of the United States. These forests should be sanctuaries for wildlife, not shooting galleries where macho types go to vent their urban frustrations. Just like humans, animals have the right to freedom and the pursuit of happiness in their own homeland. Of all the forms of hunting, trophy hunting is the most unforgivable. Imagine if it were the other way around and animals were hunting humans. Would it be fair for your grandfather to be killed because of his age and stature? That's how hunters choose their game, based on their age and dignity. The elk with the largest rack is chosen to die so its head can hang in the den of some rich hunter. Half the time the hunters don't even take the meat from the game they shoot. They just leave it to rot.

31. This argument relies primarily on which of the following techniques to make its points?

a. researched facts in support of an assertion

b. emotional assertions

c. fair and reasoned appeals to non-hunters

d. fair and reasoned appeals to hunters

32. The author is most opposed to which of the following types of hunting?

a. small game

b. large game

c. trophy

d. elk

33. By choosing the term "shooting galleries," the author implies that

a. the national forests have become dangerous for non-hunters

b. hunters should satisfy themselves by taking pictures of animals

c. hunters have an unfair advantage over prey in national forests

d. hunting licenses cost little more than the pittance paid at carnival games

Improving Streamside Wildlife Habitats
(excerpt from Habitat Extension Bulletin put out by the Wyoming
Game and Fish Department)

Riparian vegetation [the green band of vegetation along a watercourse] can help stabilize stream banks; filter sediment from surface runoff; and provide wildlife habitat, livestock forage, and scenic value. Well-developed vegetation also allows bank soils to absorb extra water during spring runoff, releasing it later during drier months, thus improving late-summer stream flows.

In many parts of the arid West, trees and shrubs are found only in riparian areas. Woody plants are very important as winter cover for many wildlife species, including upland game birds such as pheasants and turkeys. Often this winter cover is the greatest single factor limiting game bird populations. Woody vegetation also provides hiding cover and browse for many other species of birds and mammals, both game and non-game.

Dead trees ("snags") are an integral part of streamside habitats and should be left standing whenever possible. Woodpeckers, nuthatches, brown creepers, and other birds eat the insects that decompose the wood. These insects usually pose no threat to nearby living trees. Occasionally a disease organism or misuse of pesticides will weaken or kill a stand of trees. If several trees in a small area begin to die, contact your local extension agent immediately.

34. What is the effect of the word choice "riparian"?
   a. It gives the article an authoritative, scientific tone.
   b. It causes confusion, since both streams and rivers could be viewed as riparian.
   c. It seems condescending, as if the author were stooping to teach readers.
   d. It misleads readers into thinking they are getting scientific information when they are not.

35. By listing the specific birds that live in riparian areas, the author conveys a sense of
   a. urgency on behalf of endangered species
   b. the rich and varied life in such areas
   c. his or her own importance as a scientific expert
   d. poetic wonder over the variety found in nature

36. Assume that the author has done some other writing on this topic for a different audience. The other piece begins: "Remember the last time you walked along a stream? No doubt thick vegetation prevented easy progress." What is the likely effect on the reader of this opening?
   a. an aroused interest, due to the reference to the reader's personal experience
   b. resentment, due to being addressed so personally
   c. loss of interest, because the opening line makes no attempt to draw the reader in
   d. confusion, because not every reader has walked along a stream

37. The main subject of the second paragraph of this passage is
- a. the types of birds that live in riparian areas
- b. the effect of winter cover on water purity
- c. the role of trees and shrubs in riparian areas
- d. how game bird populations are affected by winter cover

38. Overall, the assertions of this passage seem to be based on
- a. rash opinion with little observation behind it
- b. deeply held emotional convictions
- c. fact derived from scientific literature
- d. inconclusive evidence gathered in field studies

39. What does the word "arid" accomplish in the first sentence of the second paragraph?
- a. It provides a sense of the generally high altitude of the West.
- b. It signifies a change in subject from the Eastern U. S. to the West.
- c. It clarifies the author's purpose to discuss non-urban areas.
- d. It clarifies the reason that trees and shrubs are found only in riparian areas.

(excerpt from "First," a short story)

First, you ought to know that I'm "only" fourteen. My mother points this out frequently. I can make decisions for myself when I'm old enough to vote, she says. Second, I should tell you that she's right—I'm not always responsible. I sometimes take the prize for a grade-A dork. Last weekend, for instance, when I was staying at Dad's, I decided it was time I learned to drive. It was Sunday morning, 7 A. M. to be exact, and I hadn't slept well thinking about this argument I'll be telling you about in a minute. Nobody was up yet in the neighborhood, and I thought there would be no harm in backing the car out of the garage and cruising around the block. But Dad has a clutch car, and the "R" on the shift handle was up on the left side, awful close to first gear, and I guess you can guess the rest.

Dad's always been understanding. He didn't say, like Mom would, "Okay, little Miss Know-It-All, you can just spend the rest of the year paying this off." He worried about what might have happened to *me*—to *me*, you see, and that made me feel more guilty than anything. Overall, I just think he'd be a better number one caregiver, if you get my drift. Of course I can't say things like that to Mom.

To her, I have to say, "But Mom, Dad's place is closer to school. I could ride my bike."

She replies, "Jennifer Lynn, you don't own a bike, because you left it in the yard and it was stolen and you haven't got the perseverance it takes to do a little work and earn the money to replace it."

40. Which description best explains the structure of the story so far?
   a. chronological, according to what happens first, second, and so on
   b. reverse chronological order, with the most recent events recorded first
   c. intentionally confused order, incorporating flashbacks to previous events
   d. according to importance, with the most significant details related first

41. What device does the author use to illustrate the narrator's feelings about her mother and father?
   a. vivid and specific visual detail
   b. rhetorical questions, which make a point but don't invite a direct answer
   c. metaphors and other figurative language
   d. contrast between the parents' typical reactions

42. The narrator attributes her inability to sleep when staying at her father's house to
   a. thinking about a disagreement with someone
   b. the uncomfortable quiet of an early Sunday morning
   c. the sore throat she had from shouting so much
   d. her accident with the car

43. The first-person point of view in this story
   a. obscures how the narrator's mind works
   b. illustrates the thoughts and personality of the narrator
   c. makes the narrator seem distant and rigid
   d. gives us direct access to the minds of all the characters

44. When the narrator says she sometimes "take[s] the prize for a grade A dork," the word choice is intended to indicate
   a. that she doesn't know proper English
   b. her age and culture
   c. that she is unable to judge her own actions
   d. that she thinks she's better than most others who might be termed "dorks"

45. From the context in the last sentence of the passage, it can be determined that the word "perseverance" most nearly means
   a. attractiveness
   b. thinking ability
   c. ability to persist
   d. love of danger

46. Overall, this narrator's tone is best described as
   a. emotional and familiar
   b. stuck up and superior
   c. argumentative and tactless
   d. pleasant and reassuring

47. In choosing to use the bike argument with her mother, the narrator is trying to appeal to her mother's
   a. compassion over her lost bike
   b. disregard for material objects
   c. laziness
   d. reason

48. The main argument the narrator has been having with her mother is over whether she should
   a. be allowed to date
   b. live with her mother or father
   c. be allowed to drive a car
   d. pay for things she breaks

49. It appears that the mother has alienated her daughter by
a. being too busy to give her the attention she needs
b. having divorced her father
c. insisting too much on reasonableness
d. valuing things over people and feelings

50. What most likely happened with the car?
a. The narrator mistook first gear for reverse and ran into the garage wall.
b. The narrator stole it from her father and drove it over to her mother's.
c. The father left it in gear, and when the narrator started it, it leapt forward into the wall.
d. The narrator attempted suicide through carbon monoxide poisoning.

ANSWER KEY

If you miss any of the answers, you can find help for that kind of question in the lesson shown to the right of the answer.

1. c. Lesson 1	**26.** d. Lesson 9
2. a. Lesson 1	**27.** c. Lesson 1
3. d. Lesson 9	**28.** a. Lessons 6 and 10
4. a. Lesson 16	**29.** d. Lesson 3
5. b. Lesson 3	**30.** d. Lesson 6
6. c. Lesson 12	**31.** b. Lesson 18
7. c. Lesson 2	**32.** c. Lesson 2
8. b. Lessons 6 and 7	**33.** c. Lesson 12
9. a. Lesson 3	**34.** a. Lesson 12
10. b. Lesson 8	**35.** b. Lesson 13
11. d. Lesson 4	**36.** a. Lesson 11
12. c. Lesson 17	**37.** c. Lesson 2
13. d. Lesson 2	**38.** c. Lesson 4
14. b. Lesson 8	**39.** d. Lesson 3
15. c. Lesson 4	**40.** c. Lessons 6, 7, and 10
16. b. Lesson 13	**41.** d. Lesson 8
17. a. Lesson 19	**42.** a. Lesson 9
18. d. Lesson 3	**43.** b. Lesson 11
19. c. Lesson 8	**44.** b. Lesson 12
20. c. Lesson 19	**45.** c. Lesson 3
21. b. Lesson 19	**46.** a. Lesson 14
22. a. Lesson 16	**47.** d. Lesson 18
23. c. Lesson 13	**48.** b. Lesson 16
24. a. Lesson 14	**49.** d. Lesson 17
25. b. Lesson 11	**50.** a. Lesson 17

BUILDING A STRONG FOUNDATION

The truth is out there." If you're an "X-Files" fan, you've heard this eerie prophesy before. When agents Mulder and Scully arrive at the scene of a crime, they want to know the *truth* about what happened. They don't let the *opinions* of assuming police officers or disbelieving witnesses sway them; they want to know what people actually *saw* happen—to witness the tangible evidence themselves. With these collected *facts*, they retire to the lab or office to draw their own conclusions. Granted, these conclusions are sometimes a bit "out of this world," but the important thing is that the conclusions are based on facts, not the opinions of others.

You may never have thought of it this way before, but critical readers are a lot like special agents. When you read, you're looking for clues, not to solve a crime, but to understand the author's meaning. What is this passage about? What is the writer saying? What is his or her message? Sometimes you may feel that authors are trying to hide their meaning from you. But no matter how complex a piece of writing may be, the author always leaves plenty of clues for the careful reader to find. Your job as a reader is to find those clues. You can do this by being a good detective, opening your eyes and asking the right questions—in other words, by reading carefully and actively.

In these first five lessons, you'll cover the basics of reading comprehension. By the end of this section, you should be able to:

- Find the basic facts in a passage
- Determine the main idea of a passage
- Determine the meaning of unfamiliar words from context
- Distinguish between fact and opinion

L·E·S·S·O·N

GETTING THE ESSENTIAL INFORMATION

1

LESSON SUMMARY

The first step in increasing your reading comprehension is to learn how to get the basic information. Like a good detective, you start with the basic facts. To get the facts, you have to be an active reader, looking for clues in what you read.

Imagine, for a moment, that you are a detective. You have just been called to the scene of a crime; a house has been robbed. What's the first thing you should do when you arrive?

a. see what's on the TV
b. check what's in the fridge
c. get the basic facts of the case

The answer, of course, is c, get the basic facts of the case: the who, what, when, where, how, and why. What happened? To whom? When? Where? How did it happen? And why?

As a reader faced with a text, you go through a similar process. The first thing you should do is establish the facts. What does this piece of writing tell you? What happens? To whom? When, where, how, and why? If you can answer these basic questions, you're on your way to really comprehending what you read. (You'll work on answering the more difficult question—"*Why* did it happen?"—in Lesson 2.)

WHAT ARE THE FACTS?

Let's start with a definition. A **fact** is:

- Something that we know for certain to have happened
- Something that we know for certain to be true
- Something that we know for certain to exist

Much of what you read, especially today in this "Information Age," is designed to provide you with facts. You may read, for example, about a new office procedure that you must follow; about how the new computer system works; about what happened at the staff meeting. If you're taking a standardized test to help you get a job, you'll probably have to answer reading comprehension questions that ask you about the facts in a passage you read. Sometimes this won't be so easy, especially when the reading is especially dense or complicated. To make it simpler, ask yourself these questions as you read: What facts am I expected to know? What am I to learn or be aware of? What happened? What is true? What exists?

PRACTICE PASSAGE 1

Jump right into the task of finding facts. The brief passage below is similar to something you might see in a newspaper. Read the passage carefully, and then answer the questions that follow. Remember, careful reading is active reading (see the Introduction), so mark up the text as you go. Underline key words and ideas; circle and define any unfamiliar words or phrases; record your reactions and questions in the margins.

On Tuesday, August 30, Mr. Blank, a prominent local citizen, arrived home from work to find that his apartment had been robbed. The thieves somehow managed to slip past building security at 131 West Elm Street with nearly all of Mr. Blank's belongings. In fact, the thieves left behind nothing but a stack of old *Home Decorator* magazines and a can of pork and beans. The robbery was reported by Mr. Blank's neighbor, who found Mr. Blank unconscious in his doorway. Apparently, Mr. Blank was so shocked by the robbery that he fainted. His neighbor immediately called an ambulance and then the police. Mr. Blank is now staying with relatives and is offering a reward of $25,000 for any information leading to the arrest of the thieves.

1. What happened to Mr. Blank?

2. When did it happen?

3. Where did it happen?

4. How did Mr. Blank react?

5. Who called the police?

6. What was left in the apartment?

Remember, good reading is active reading. Did you mark up the passage? If so, it may have looked something like this:

when *who* *standing out; widely & popularly known*

On Tuesday, August 30, Mr. Blank, a (prominent) local citizen, arrived home from work to find that his apartment had been robbed. The thieves somehow managed to slip past building security at 131 West Elm Street with nearly all of Mr. Blank's belongings. In fact, the thieves left behind nothing but a stack of old *Home Decorator* magazines and a can of pork and beans. The robbery was reported by Mr. Blank's neighbor, who found Mr. Blank unconscious in his doorway. Apparently, Mr. Blank was so shocked by the robbery that he fainted. His neighbor immediately called an ambulance and then the police. Mr. Blank is now staying with relatives and is offering a reward of $25,000 for any information leading to the arrest of the thieves.

how did they manage this?

interesting detail.

who else was involved

What happened – robbery

where

Wow!

lots of $!

You'll notice that the answers to the questions have all been underlined, because these are the key words and ideas in this passage. But here are the answers in a more conventional form:

1. What happened to Mr. Blank? *His apartment was robbed.*

2. When did it happen? *Sometime while Mr. Blank was at work on Tuesday, August 30.*

3. Where did it happen? *131 West Elm Street.*

4. How did Mr. Blank react? *He fainted.*

5. Who called the police? *Mr. Blank's neighbor.*

6. What was left in the apartment? *Some old Home Decorator magazines and a can of pork and beans.*

Notice that these questions went beyond the basic who, what, when, and where to include some of the details, like what was left in the apartment. This is because details in reading comprehension, as well as in detective work, can be very important clues that may help answer the remaining questions: who did it, how, and why.

PRACTICE PASSAGE 2

Here's another passage, this time something a little more like what someone might see at work. Read the passage carefully and answer the questions that follow:

To: All New Employees
From: Human Resources

In order for your first paycheck to be processed, we must have a number of documents completed and in our files. Once these documents are in our hands, you will be entered into our payroll system. These documents include: a completed company application; a W-4 form; an I-9 form; a Confidentiality Agreement, if applicable; an emergency contact sheet; and a copy of your resume. You should be sure all of these documents are filled out within your first week of work. In addition, we will need the following documents from you for your file to be complete: two letters of recommendation from previous employers, a high school and college transcript, and an insurance coverage application. We request that you complete your file within your first month of employment.

---

7. What papers must new employees have on file? List them below.

8. In your list above, circle the items that employees must have on file in order to get paid.

9. When should these circled items be completed?

10. When must the rest of the file be completed?

11. True or False: Everyone must sign a Confidentiality Agreement.

Before you look at the answers, look at the next page to see how you might have marked up the passage to highlight the important information.

To: All New Employees
From: Human Resources

In order for your first paycheck to be processed, we must have a number of documents completed and in our files. Once these documents are in our hands, you will be entered into our payroll system. These documents include: [a completed company application; a W-4 form; an I-9 form; a Confidentiality Agreement, if applicable; an emergency contact sheet; and a copy of your resume.] You should be sure all of these documents are filled out within your first week of work. In addition, we will need the following documents from you for your file to be complete: [two letters of recommendation from previous employers, a high school and college transcript, and an insurance coverage application.] We request that you complete your file within your first month of employment.

Important deadline! (handwritten annotation)

Official copy of a student's educational record (handwritten annotation)

Documents I need in order to get paid (handwritten annotation)

Documents I need to complete file (handwritten annotation)

Deadline for completing file (handwritten annotation)

With a marked-up text like this, it's very easy to find the answers.

7. What papers must new employees have on file?

   (Company application)
   (W-4 form)
   (I-9 form)
   (Confidentiality Agreement (if applicable))
   (Emergency contact sheet)
   (Resume)
   Two letters of recommendation
   High school and college transcripts
   Insurance coverage application

8. In the list above, the items that employees must have on file in order to get paid are circled.

9. When should these circled items be completed? *Within the employee's first week of work.*

10. When must the rest of the file be completed? *Within the employee's first month of work.*

11. True or False: Everyone must sign a Confidentiality Agreement. *False; only those for whom it is "applicable."*

PRACTICE PASSAGE 3

Now look at one more short passage. Again, read carefully and then answer the questions that follow.

Today's postal service is more efficient and reliable than ever before. Mail that used to take months to move by horse and by foot now moves around the country in days or hours by truck, train, and plane. First class mail usually moves from New York City to Los Angeles in three days or less. If your letter or package is urgent, the U.S. Postal Service offers Priority Mail and Express Mail services. Priority Mail is guaranteed to go anywhere in the U.S. in two days or less. Express Mail will get your package there overnight.

12. Who or what is this passage about?

13. How was mail transported in the past?

14. How is mail transported now?

15. How long does first class mail take?

16. How long does Priority Mail take?

17. How long does Express Mail take?

Once again, here's how you might have marked up this passage:

Today's postal service is more efficient and reliable than ever before. Mail *What a long time!* that used to take <u>months</u> to move by <u>horse</u> and by <u>foot</u> now moves around the *then →* country in days or hours by <u>truck, train, and plane</u>. First class <u>mail</u> usually moves *now →* from New York City to Los Angeles in three days or less. If your letter or package is urgent, the U.S. Postal Service offers <u>Priority Mail</u> and <u>Express Mail</u> services. Priority Mail is guaranteed to go anywhere in the U.S. in two days or less. Express Mail will get your package there overnight.

Are there other services?

*3 services listed—
First class–3days
Priority–2 days
Express–Overnight
Fastest*

You can see how marking up a text helps make it easier to understand the information a passage conveys.

12. Who or what is this passage about? *The U.S. Postal Service.*

13. How was mail transported in the past? *By horse and foot.*

14. How is mail transported now? *By truck, train, and plane.*

15. How long does first class mail take? *Three days or less.*

16. How long does Priority Mail take? *Two days or less.*

17. How long does Express Mail take? *Overnight.*

SUMMARY

Active reading is the first essential step to comprehension. Why? Because active reading forces you to really *see* what you're reading, to look closely at what's there. Like a detective who arrives at the scene of a crime, if you look carefully and ask the right questions (who, what, when, where, how, and why), you're on your way to really comprehending what you read.

Skill Building Until Next Time

Below are some suggestions for practicing the skills covered in this chapter throughout the day and even the rest of the week. Try them!

- **Mark up** everything you read throughout the day—the newspaper, a memo, a letter from a friend. Underline the key terms and ideas; circle and look up any unfamiliar words; write your reactions and questions in the margins. If possible, share these reactions with the writer and see if you can get answers to your questions.

- Develop a **"detective's eye."** Begin to notice things around you. Look at the details on people's faces; notice the architectural details of the buildings you enter. The more observant you are in daily life, the more enriched your life will be and the easier it will be to comprehend what you read.

L·E·S·S·O·N

FINDING THE MAIN IDEA

2

LESSON SUMMARY

A detective finds the facts to determine "whodunit" and what the motive was. A reader determines the facts not only for their own sake but also to find out why the author is writing: What's the main idea? This lesson shows you how to determine the main idea of what you read.

hen Lesson 1 talked about establishing the facts—the who, what, when, where, and how—it omitted one very important question: Why? Now you're ready to tackle that all-important question. Just as there's a motive behind every crime, there's also a "motive" behind every piece of writing.

All writing is communication: A writer writes to convey his or her thoughts to an audience, the reader; you. Just as you have something to say (a motive) when you pick up the phone to call someone, writers have something to say (a motive) when they pick up a pen or pencil to write. Where a detective might ask, "Why did the butler do it?" the reader might ask, "Why did the author write this? What idea is he or she trying to convey?" What you're really asking is, "What is the writer's main idea?"

Finding the main idea is much like finding the motive of the crime. It's the motive of the crime (the *why*) that usually determines the other factors (the *who, what, when, where,* and *how*). Similarly, in writing, the main idea also determines the *who, what, when,* and *where* the writer will write about, as well as *how* he or she will write.

SUBJECT VS. MAIN IDEA

There's a difference between the *subject* of a piece of writing and its *main idea.* To see the difference, look again at the passage about the postal system. Don't skip over it! You read it in Lesson 1, but please read it again, and read it carefully.

> Today's postal service is more efficient and reliable than ever before. Mail that used to take months to move by horse and by foot now moves around the country in days or hours by truck, train, and plane. First class mail usually moves from New York City to Los Angeles in three days or less. If your letter or package is urgent, the U.S. Postal Service offers Priority Mail and Express Mail services. Priority Mail is guaranteed to go anywhere in the U.S. in two days or less. Express Mail will get your package there overnight.

You might be asked on a standardized test, "What is the main idea of this reading?"

For the passage above, you might be tempted to answer: "The post office."

But you'd be wrong.

This passage is *about* the post office, yes—but "the post office" is not the main idea of the passage. "The post office" is merely the *subject* of the passage (*who* or *what* the passage is about). The main idea must say something *about* this subject. The main idea of a text is usually an *assertion* about the subject. An assertion is a statement that requires evidence ("proof") to be accepted as true.

The main idea of a passage is an assertion about its subject, but it is something more: It is the idea that also holds together or controls the passage. The other sentences and ideas in the passage will all relate to that main idea and serve as "evidence" that the assertion is true. You might think of the main idea as a net that is cast over the other sentences. The main idea must be general enough to hold all of these ideas together.

Thus, the main idea of a passage is:

- An assertion about the subject
- The general idea that controls or holds together the paragraph or passage

Look at the postal service paragraph once more. You know what the subject is: "the post office." Now, see if you can determine the main idea. Read the passage again and look for the idea that makes an assertion about the postal service *and* holds together or controls the whole paragraph. Then answer the following question:

1. Which of the following sentences best summarizes the main idea of the passage?
   a. Express Mail is a good way to send urgent mail.
   b. Mail service today is more effective and dependable.
   c. First class mail usually takes three days or less.

Because **a** is specific—it tells us *only* about Express Mail—it cannot be the main idea. It does not encompass the rest of the sentences in the paragraph—it doesn't cover Priority Mail or first class mail. Answer **c** is also very specific. It tells us only about first class mail, so it, too, cannot be the main idea.

But **b**—"Mail service today is more effective and dependable"—*is* general enough to encompass the whole passage. And the rest of the sentences *support* the idea that this sentence asserts: Each sentence offers "proof" that the postal service today is indeed more efficient and reliable. Thus, the writer's motive is to tell us about the efficiency and reliability of today's postal service.

TOPIC SENTENCES

You'll notice that in the paragraph about the postal service, the main idea is expressed clearly in the first sentence: "Today's postal service is more efficient and reliable than ever before." A sentence, such as this one, that clearly expresses the main idea of a paragraph or passage is often called a *topic sentence*.

In many cases, as in the postal service paragraph, you will find the topic sentence at the beginning of the paragraph. You will also frequently find it at the end. Less often, but on occasion, the topic sentence may be found in the middle of the passage. Whatever the case may be, the topic sentence—like "Today's postal service is more efficient and reliable than ever before"—is an assertion, and it needs "proof." The proof is found in the facts and ideas that make up the rest of the passage. (Not all passages provide such a clear topic sentence that states the main idea. Less obvious passages will come up in later lessons.)

PRACTICE IN IDENTIFYING TOPIC SENTENCES

Remember that a topic sentence is a clear statement of the main idea of a passage; it must be general enough to encompass all of the ideas in that passage, and it usually makes an assertion about the subject of that passage. Knowing all that, you can answer the following question even without reading a passage.

Practice 1

2. Which of the following sentences is general enough to be a topic sentence?
   a. UNIX is one of the most common computer languages.
   b. There are many different computer languages.
   c. An old computer language is BASIC.
   d. Most IBM computers use OS/2.

The answer is **b**, "There are many different computer languages." Answers **a**, **c**, and **d** are all specific examples of what is said in **b**, so they are not general enough to be topic sentences.

Practice 2

Now look at the following paragraph. Underline the sentence that expresses the main idea, and notice how the other sentences work to support that main idea.

Erik always played cops and robbers when he was a boy; now, he's a police officer. Suzanne always played school as a little girl; today, she is a high school math teacher. Kara always played store; today, she owns a chain of retail clothing shops. Long before they are faced with the question, "What do you want to be when you grow up?" some lucky people know exactly what they want to do with their lives.

Which sentence did you underline? You should have underlined the *last* sentence: "Long before they are faced with that question 'What do you want to be when you grow up?' some lucky people know exactly what they want to do with their lives." This sentence is a good topic sentence; it expresses the idea that holds together the whole paragraph. The first three sentences—about Erik, Suzanne, and Kara—are *specific examples* of these lucky people. Notice that this time the topic sentence is found at the *end* of the paragraph.

Practice 3

Among the eight sentences below are *two* topic sentences. The other sentences are supporting sentences. Circle the two topic sentences. Then write the numbers of the supporting sentences that go with each topic sentence.

1. Furthermore, government employees receive terrific heath-care coverage.

2. Some police officer duties, like writing reports, have no risk at all.

3. For example, government employees have more paid holidays than employees of private companies.

4. Not all police duties are dangerous.

5. Others, like traffic duty, put police officers at very little risk.

6. Government employees enjoy numerous benefits.

7. Still other duties, like investigating accidents, leave officers free of danger.

8. In addition, government employees are well compensated for overtime hours.

Sentences 4 and 6 are the *two* topic sentences because both make an assertion about a general subject. The supporting sentences for topic sentence 4, "Not all police duties are dangerous," are sentences 2, 5, and 7. The supporting sentences for topic sentence 6, "Government employees enjoy numerous benefits," are the remaining sentences: 1, 3, and 8.

Here's how they look as paragraphs:

Not all police duties are dangerous. Some duties, like writing reports, have no risk at all. Others, like traffic duty, offer very little risk. Still other duties, like investigating accidents, leave officers free of danger.

Government employees enjoy numerous benefits. For example, they have more paid holidays than employees of private companies. In addition, they are well compensated for overtime hours. Furthermore, they receive terrific heath-care coverage.

You might have noticed the supporting sentences in the first paragraph about police duties begin with the following words: *some, others,* and *still other.* These words are often used to introduce examples. The second paragraph uses different words, but they have the same function: *for example, in addition,* and *furthermore.* If a sentence begins with such a word or phrase, that is a good indication it is *not* a topic sentence—because it is providing a specific example.

Here are some words and phrases often used to introduce specific examples:

for example	in particular
for instance	some
in addition	others
furthermore	

If you're having trouble finding the main idea of a paragraph, you might try eliminating the sentences that you know contain supporting evidence.

SUMMARY

Now you can answer the last of the questions—the *why.* What is the writer's motive? What's the main idea he or she wants to convey? By finding the sentence that makes an assertion about the subject of the paragraph and that encompasses the other sentences in the paragraph, you can uncover the author's motive.

Skill Building Until Next Time

■ A paragraph, by definition, is a group of sentences about the same idea. As you read today and the rest of the week, notice how texts are divided into paragraphs. What idea holds each paragraph together? Can you identify any **topic sentences**?

■ Formulate **topic sentences** about things that you come across in your day. Make assertions about these people, places, and things. For example, you may eat in the cafeteria every day. Make an *assertion* about it: "This cafeteria needs remodeling," for example. Or, make an assertion about a co-worker: "June is a very hard worker," you might say. Then, support your assertions. What "evidence" could you supply for your paragraph? Why do you say the cafeteria needs remodeling? Is there paint peeling off the walls? Is it still decorated '60s style? Is it not wheelchair accessible? What evidence do you have that June is a hard worker? Is she always at her computer? Does she ask informed questions in staff meetings? Does she look like she needs more sleep?

L·E·S·S·O·N 3

DEFINING VOCABULARY IN CONTEXT

LESSON SUMMARY

An active reader looks up unfamiliar words. But what if you don't have a dictionary? In a testing situation (or, for that matter, if you're reading on the bus) you almost certainly won't be able to look up words you don't know. Instead, you can use the context to help you determine the meaning.

ometimes in your reading you come across words or phrases that are unfamiliar to you. You might be lucky enough to have a dictionary handy to look up that word or phrase, but what if you don't? How can you understand what you're reading if you don't know what all of the words mean? The answer is that you can use the rest of the passage, the *context*, to help you understand the new words.

FINDING MEANING FROM CONTEXT

Imagine you are a Hiring Supervisor at a large company. You have just received the following memorandum from the Human Resources Department. Read it carefully, marking it up as you go—but **don't** look up any unfamiliar words or phrases in a dictionary.

As you know, all new employees must have a Hiring Approval Form with salary specifications on file before they can be paid. In recent months several new employees have had their paychecks delayed because their Hiring Supervisors were remiss in filing the Hiring Approval Forms on time. Consequently, we are instituting a new policy. Beginning next week, if a Hiring Approval Form is not filed with Human Resources within one week of an employee's start date, that employee's first paycheck will be deducted from his or her Hiring Supervisor's paycheck. This amount will not be reimbursed unless the Hiring Supervisor submits the Hiring Approval Form within the following week. We're sorry if this seems like a draconian policy, but it is our only way to assure prompt payment of new employees.

As you read, you may have circled some words that are unfamiliar. Did you circle *remiss* and *draconian*? If so, don't look them up in a dictionary yet. If you do a little detective work, you can figure out what these words mean by looking carefully at how they are used in the paragraph.

WHAT DOES *REMISS* MEAN?

Start with *remiss*. How is this word used?

In recent months several new employees have had their paychecks delayed because their Hiring Supervisors were *remiss* in filing the Hiring Approval Forms on time.

Even if you have no idea what *remiss* means, you can still tell something about the word by how it is used, by examining the words and ideas surrounding it. This is called determining word meaning through **context**.

Like detectives looking for clues at a crime scene, we must look at the passage for clues that will tell us what this word means.

So, given the sentence we have here, what can we tell about *remiss?* Well, because the Hiring Supervisors were *remiss*, several new employees didn't get their paychecks on time. That immediately tells us that *remiss* is *not* a good thing to be.

Furthermore, we know from this sentence that the Hiring Approval Forms must be filed by the Hiring Supervisors. That tells us that Hiring Supervisors were not doing something they were supposed to do, doesn't it? And as a result, the rest of the paragraph tells us, Hiring Supervisors will now be penalized for not filing the Hiring Approval Forms. Now you can take a pretty good guess at the meaning of *remiss*.

1. The Hiring Supervisors were remiss about the Hiring Approval Forms because they were
   a. on time, prompt
   b. negligent, irresponsible
   c. incorrect, wrong

The correct answer, of course, is **b**. It certainly can't be **a**, because you know that the forms were late (the forms were not "on time"). Besides, you know *remiss* must mean something negative, since the Hiring Supervisors who continue to be remiss will be punished. Answer **c** is negative, but it doesn't make sense in the context of the sentence, which tells you the issue is time. Furthermore, you know **b** is the correct answer because you can substitute both *irresponsible* and *negligent* in the sentence instead of *remiss* and they both make sense.

Review: Finding Facts

Here's a quick review of what you learned in Lesson 1. If you're a Hiring Supervisor, you know that now you must be sure to get Hiring Approval Forms in *on time*. But when is *on time?*

2. When must the Hiring Approval Form be in for the new employee to be paid on time?
   a. within one week of the employee's start date
   b. by next week
   c. within one month of the hiring approval

A quick check of the facts in the paragraph will tell you the answer: **a**, within one week of the employee's start date.

WHAT DOES *DRACONIAN* MEAN?

Look again at the sentence in which *draconian* is used:

We're sorry if this seems like a *draconian* policy, but it is our only way to assure prompt payment of new employees.

Again, even if you have no idea what *draconian* means (and no, it has nothing to do with Dracula!), you can still tell what kind of word it is by the way it is used. You can, for example, answer this question:

3. *Draconian* is a
   a. positive word
   b. negative word

The answer, of course, is that it is a negative word. How can you tell? Well, there's one very obvious clue in the sentence: "We're sorry." Why would the memo writers be sorry if *draconian* was something to be happy about?

Okay, now that you've established that *draconian* is not something good, figure out *why* by determining exactly what it means. Your first clue to the meaning of *draconian* was "We're sorry." What other clues can you find? Look at how *draconian* is being used in this sentence: It is used to describe the new policy explained in the memo. And what is this new policy? The Hiring Supervisor's pay will be deducted if he or she doesn't make sure the Hiring Approval Form is completed within one week of a new employee's start date. And if the Hiring Approval Form still isn't filed by the end of the next week, the Hiring Supervisor will *not* be reimbursed. That should give you a pretty good idea of what *draconian* means.

4. A *draconian* policy is one that is
   a. mismanaged, unorganized
   b. lenient, light
   c. drastic, severe
   d. smart, wise

The correct answer, of course, is **c**, "drastic, severe." It can't be **b** or **d**, because these are positive things that the writers of the memo wouldn't be sorry for. And **a** is not an appropriate answer because, as you can see, the policy is quite clear; you know exactly what form needs to be on file, who's responsible for it, and what happens if the form is not filed. In addition, you can tell that **c** is the right answer because docking someone's pay without reimbursement because of missing paperwork certainly is a harsh measure.

By the way, the word *draconian* comes from the ancient Greek lawmaker, Draco, who wrote particularly harsh laws with severe penalties.

How Much Context Do You Need?

In the previous example, you would still be able to understand the main message of the memorandum even if you didn't know—or couldn't figure out—the meaning of *remiss* and *draconian*. In some cases, however, your understanding of a passage depends on your understanding of a particular word or phrase. Can you understand the following sentence, for example, without knowing what *adversely* means?

The new policy will *adversely* affect all employees.

If you're an employee, you certainly want to know how you're going to be affected. What does *adversely* mean? Is it something good or bad? As good a detective as you may be, there simply aren't enough clues in this sentence to tell you what this word means. But a passage with more information will give you what you need to determine meaning from context.

The new policy will *adversely* affect all employees. It will freeze their pay, limit their vacation time, and reduce their health benefits.

5. In the passage, *adversely* most nearly means
   a. mildly, slightly
   b. regularly, steadily
   c. negatively, unfavorably
   d. immediately, swiftly

The correct answer is **c**, "negatively, unfavorably." The brief passage now tells you exactly what the policy will do to the employees: It will freeze their pay, limit their vacations, and reduce their benefits. It certainly is not **a**, a slight or mild change, nor is it **b**, a regular or steady change. And you don't know if it is an immediate or swift change (**d**), because the sentence says nothing about the time frame in which this change will take place. Remember, good detectives don't make assumptions they can't support with facts; and there are no facts in this sentence to support the assumption that the changes will take place immediately. Thus, **c** is the best answer.

You may also have noticed that *adversely* is very similar to the word *adversary*. And if you know that an *adversary* is a hostile opponent or enemy, then you know that *adversely* cannot be something positive. Or, if you know the word *adversity*—hardship or misfortune—then you know that *adversely* must mean something negative or difficult. All of these words share the same root—*advers*. Only the endings change.

PRACTICE
Read the following passages and determine the meaning of the words from their context. The answers appear immediately after the questions.

Although social work is not a particularly *lucrative* career, I wouldn't do anything else. Knowing I'm helping others is far more important to me than money.

6. *Lucrative* means
   a. highly profitable
   b. highly rewarding
   c. highly exciting

When you are in an interview, try not to show any *overt* signs that you are nervous. Don't shift in your chair, shake, or stutter.

7. *Overt* means
   a. embarrassing, awkward
   b. subtle, suggestive
   c. obvious, not hidden

By the time our staff meeting ended at 8:00, I was *ravenous.* I had skipped lunch and hadn't eaten since breakfast.

8. *Ravenous* means
   a. like a raven, bird-like
   b. extremely hungry, greedy for food
   c. exhausted, ready for bed

Answers

6. a. The writer says money is not important to him. If money is not an issue, it is okay that social work is not *highly profitable,* that it doesn't earn a lot of money.

7. c. Shifting, shaking, and stuttering are all *obvious, not hidden* signs of nervousness. They are not **b,** subtle or suggestive; and though they may make the interviewee feel **a,** embarrassed or awkward, the signs themselves are not embarrassing or awkward.

8. b. Because the writer hadn't eaten since breakfast, she is *extremely hungry, greedy for food.* She may also be **c,** exhausted, but the context tells us that this word has something to do with eating.

SUMMARY

Being able to determine the meaning of unfamiliar words from their context is an essential skill for reading comprehension. Sometimes there will be unfamiliar words whose meaning you can't figure out without a dictionary. But more often than not, a careful look at the context will give you enough clues to meaning.

Skill Building Until Next Time

- Circle any unfamiliar words you come across today and the rest of the week. Instead of looking them up in a dictionary, try to figure out the meanings of these words from their context. Then look them up in a dictionary to make sure you are correct.

- Begin a vocabulary list of the words you look up as you work your way through this book. Many people feel insecure about their reading and writing skills because they have a limited vocabulary. The more words you know, the easier it will be to understand what others are saying and to express what you have to say. By writing these new words down, you'll help seal them in your memory.

THE DIFFERENCE BETWEEN FACT AND OPINION

4

LESSON SUMMARY

In order to make sense of what you read, you have to be able to tell whether you're reading fact or opinion. This lesson tells you how to distinguish what someone knows for certain from what someone believes.

hat's the difference between fact and opinion, and what does it matter, anyway? It matters a great deal, especially when it comes to reading comprehension.

During your life, you'll be exposed to a wide variety of literature, ranging from analytical articles based on cold hard facts to fictional novels that arise wholly from the author's imagination. However, much of what you read will be a mixture of facts and the author's opinions. Part of becoming a critical reader means realizing that opinions are not evidence; for opinions to be valid, they must be supported by cold, hard facts:

- Things *known* for certain to have happened
- Things *known* for certain to be true
- Things *known* for certain to exist

    Opinions, on the other hand, are:

- Things *believed* to have happened
- Things *believed* to be true
- Things *believed* to exist

As you can see, the key difference between fact and opinion lies in the difference between *believing* and *knowing*. Opinions may be based on facts, but they are still what we *think*, not what we *know*. Opinions are debatable; facts are not.

USING FACTS TO SUPPORT OPINIONS

Reasonable opinions are those that are *based on fact*; and indeed, that is what much of writing is: the writer's opinion (an assertion about his or her subject) supported by facts or other evidence.

Think about the topic sentences you formed after you finished Lesson 2. Did you form a topic sentence about a classmate, for example? Perhaps you made an assertion like this:

James is a terrific boss.

This sentence is a good topic sentence; it's an assertion about the subject, James. And it is also an opinion. It is, after all, debatable; someone could just as easily take the opposite position and say:

James is a terrible boss.

This is another good topic sentence, and it's another opinion. Now, a good writer will show his or her readers that this opinion is *valid* by supporting it with facts. For example:

James is a terrific boss. He always asks us how we're doing. He lets us leave early or come in late when we have to take care of our children. He always gives holiday bonuses. And he offers tuition reimbursement for any course, even if it has nothing to do with our position.

Notice how the topic sentence states an opinion, whereas the rest of the sentences support that opinion

with facts about how James treats his employees. Now, that is a much more effective paragraph than something like this:

James is a terrible boss. I really don't like him. He just can't get along with people. And he has stupid ideas about politics.

Why is the first paragraph so much better? Because it's not just opinion. It's opinion supported by fact, evidence. The second paragraph is all opinion. Every sentence is debatable; every sentences tells us what the author *thinks* is true, but not what is *known* to be true. The author of the second paragraph doesn't provide any evidence to support why he thinks that James is such a lousy boss. As a result, we're not likely to take his opinion very seriously.

In the first paragraph, on the other hand, the writer offers concrete evidence for why she thinks James is a great boss. After the initial opinion, she provides facts—specific things James does (which can be verified by other observers) that make him a good boss. You may still not agree that James is a great boss, but at least you can see exactly why this writer thinks so.

DISTINGUISHING FACT FROM OPINION

When you read academic materials very often you will have to distinguish between fact and opinion—between what the writer thinks and how the writer supports what he or she thinks, between what is proven to be true and what needs to be proved.

A good test for whether something is a fact or opinion might be to ask yourself, "Can this statement be debated? Is this known for certain to be true?" If you answer *yes* to the first question, you have an opinion; if you answer *yes* to the second, you have a fact.

PRACTICE 1

Try these questions on the following statements. Read them carefully, and then write F in the blank if the statement is a fact and O if it is an opinion. The answers appear right after the questions.

_____ 1. The Olympics are held every two years.

_____ 2. The Olympics are really fun to watch.

_____ 3. The Olympics should be held every year.

_____ 4. The 1996 Summer Olympics were held in Atlanta, Georgia.

_____ 5. The long jump is the most exciting Olympic event.

Answers

1. Fact
2. Opinion
3. Opinion
4. Fact
5. Opinion

PRACTICE 2

Now try the same exercise but with a complete paragraph. Underline the facts and use a highlighter or colored pen to highlight the opinions. Be careful—you may find fact and opinion together in the same sentence. When you've finished, you can check your answers against the marked passage that follows.

There are many different ways to invest your money to provide for a financially secure future. Many people invest in stocks and bonds, but I think good old-fashioned savings accounts and CDs (certificates of deposit) are the best way to invest your hard-earned money. Stocks and bonds are often risky, and it doesn't make sense to risk losing the money you've worked so hard for. True, regular savings accounts and CDs can't make you a millionaire overnight or provide the high returns some stock investments do. But by the same token, savings accounts and CDs are fully insured and provide steady, secure interest on your money. That makes a whole lot of cents.

Answers

How did you do? Was it easy to distinguish between the facts and the opinions? Here's what your marked-up passage should look like. The facts are underlined and the opinions are in boldface type.

There are many different ways to invest your money to provide for a financially secure future. Many people invest in stocks and bonds, **but I think good old-fashioned savings accounts and CDs (certificates of deposit) are the best way to invest your hard-earned money.** Stocks and bonds are often risky, **and it doesn't make sense to risk losing the money you've worked so hard for.** True, regular savings accounts and CDs can't make you a millionaire overnight or provide the high returns some stock investments do. But by the same token, savings accounts and CDs are fully insured and provide steady, secure interest on your money. **That makes a whole lot of cents.**

PRACTICE 3

To strengthen your ability to distinguish between fact and opinion, try this. Take a fact, such as:

FACT: *Wednesday is the fourth day of the week.*

Now, turn it into an opinion. Make it something debatable, like this:

OPINION: *Wednesday is the longest day of the week.*

Here's another example:

FACT: *People insured by an HMO can only choose from doctors on that HMO plan.*

OPINION: *People insured by HMOs should be able to choose any doctor they wish.*

Now you try. Some suggested answers come after the questions.

6. **FACT:** *In the United States, you must be at least 21 years of age to drink alcohol.*

   OPINION:

7. **FACT:** *There have been many proposals recently for a flat income tax.*

   OPINION:

8. **FACT:** *Affirmative action programs have recently been eliminated.*

   OPINION:

9. FACT: *Many companies have dress-down days on Fridays.*

OPINION:

10. FACT: *Several states have recently raised their highway speed limits from 55 miles per hour to 65 miles per hour or more.*

OPINION:

All people who earn more than $100,000 a year should have a flat tax of 25 percent; people who earn less should not be taxed at all.

8. Affirmative action was a terrific program that should not have been eliminated.
It's about time we got rid of affirmative action.

9. Dress-down days improve employee morale.
Dress-down days make workers less productive.
Companies should allow their employees to dress however they wish.

10. Speed limits should remain 55 miles per hour.
There should be no speed limit at all.

Answers

There are, of course, many opinions you could form from these subjects. Here are some possible answers:

6. The legal drinking age should be 18.
There should be no age requirement for drinking alcohol.
You should not be able to drink alcohol until you're 25.

7. There should be a flat income tax of 20 percent.
A flat income tax rate would be disastrous.

SUMMARY

Being able to differentiate between fact and opinion is a very important skill. Like a detective, you need to know the difference between what people *think* and what people *know*, between what people *believe* to be true and what has been *proven* to be true. Then you will be able to see whether writers support their opinions, and, if they do, how they do it. Then you will be able to judge for yourself the validity of those opinions.

Skill Building Until Next Time

- Listen carefully to what people say today and try to determine whether they are stating a fact or expressing an opinion. When they offer opinions, do they support them?
- As you come across facts and opinions today, practice turning them into their opposites; make facts out of opinions and opinions out of facts.

L·E·S·S·O·N

PUTTING IT ALL TOGETHER

5

LESSON SUMMARY

This lesson reviews what you learned in Lessons 1–4: getting the facts, finding the main idea, determining what words mean in context, and distinguishing between fact and opinion. In this lesson, you'll get vital practice in using all four skills at once.

In order to solve a crime, a detective cannot *just* get the facts of the case, *just* discover the motive, *just* decipher difficult clues, or *just* distinguish between fact and opinion. To be successful, a detective must do all of these things at once. Similarly, reading really can't be broken down into these separate tasks. Reading comprehension comes from employing all of these strategies at once. So this lesson gives you the opportunity to put all these strategies together and take your reading comprehension skills to the next level.

REVIEW: WHAT YOU'VE LEARNED SO FAR

These are the strategies you studied in the past four lessons:

- **Lesson 1: Finding the facts in what you read.** You practiced looking for the basic information that was being conveyed in the paragraphs: the who, what, when, where, and how.
- **Lesson 2: Finding the main idea.** You learned about topic sentences and how they express an assertion about the subject of the paragraph. You saw how the main idea must be general enough to encompass all of the other sentences in the paragraph; it is the thought that controls the paragraph, and the other sentences work to support that main idea.
- **Lesson 3: Determining the meaning of words from context.** You practiced looking for clues to meaning in the words and sentences surrounding the unfamiliar word or phrase.
- **Lesson 4: Distinguishing between fact and opinion.** You learned that a fact is something *known* to be true, whereas an opinion is something *believed* to be true. You practiced distinguishing between the two and saw how good paragraphs use facts to support opinions.

If any of these terms or strategies sound unfamiliar to you, STOP. Take a few minutes to review whatever lesson is unclear.

PRACTICE

In this lesson, you will sharpen your reading comprehension skills by using all of the above strategies at once. This will become more natural to you as your reading skills develop.

PRACTICE PASSAGE 1

Begin by looking at the following paragraph. Remember to read actively; mark up the text as you go. Then answer the questions. An example of how to mark up the passage, as well as the answers to the questions, follow the questions.

Following proper procedure is important in any job. But in no job is following proper procedure more important than in police work. In police work, not following proper procedure—like not handling evidence properly—can cause an officer to ruin a case by destroying an important clue. Later, the officer may be unable to convict the perpetrator in court because of mishandled evidence. Furthermore, not following proper procedure at the scene of an accident or hold-up, for example, could cause innocent people to get hurt. Most importantly, not following proper procedure in dangerous situations like robberies in progress and high-speed chases can cost an officer his or her life.

1. What is the subject of this passage?

2. According to the passage, which of the following consequences can happen to a police officer who doesn't follow proper procedure? (Circle all correct answers.)
a. lose his or her job
b. ruin the court case
c. be unable to solve the case
d. get a reduction in pay
e. lose his or her life
f. cause others to get hurt
g. get transferred

3. A *perpetrator* is
a. a victim of a crime
b. a committer of a crime
c. an investigator of a crime
d. the object stolen

4. Which of the following best summarizes the main idea of the passage?
a. You will get fired if you don't follow proper procedure.
b. A police officer's life depends upon proper procedure.
c. Police officers more than anyone else must follow proper procedure.

5. True or False: "But in no job is following proper procedure more important than in police work" is a topic sentence.

6. True or False: "But in no job is following proper procedure more important than in police work" is an opinion.

Marking Practice Passage 1

Before you check the answers, look again at the paragraph. Did you mark it up? If so, it may look something like this:

Following proper procedure is important in any job. But in no job is following proper procedure more important than in police work. In police work, not following proper procedure—like not handling evidence properly—can cause an officer to ruin a case by destroying an important clue. Later, the officer may be unable to convict the (perpetrator) in court because of mishandled evidence. Furthermore, not following proper procedure at the scene of an accident or hold up, for example, could cause innocent people to get hurt. Most importantly, not following proper procedure in dangerous situations like robberies in progress and high-speed chases can cost an officer his or her life.

main idea

What can happen–
–ruin a case
(destroy clue)
–mishandle evidence
(unable to convict)
–hurt innocent people
–get killed

perpetrator: person who carried out or commits a crime

Answers

1. The subject of the paragraph is *following proper police procedure*. Remember, the subject of a passage is who or what the passage is about.

2. b, c, e, f. These results are all mentioned in the passage. A police officer who doesn't follow proper procedure may lose his or her job (**a**), get a reduction in pay (**d**), or get transferred (**g**), but none of these consequences are mentioned *in the paragraph itself*.

Remember, you're looking for the facts that the *author* has provided. It is extremely important, especially in test situations, not to put in an answer that isn't there in the text. *Logic* may tell you that an officer who doesn't follow proper procedure may lose his or her job, but the paragraph doesn't tell you this. Like a good detective, you need to stick to the facts of the case: what's in the passage before you. Any assumption that you make about a passage must be grounded in evidence found *in that passage itself.*

3. b. A *perpetrator* is a person who commits a crime. The most obvious clue is the way the word is used in the sentence: "the officer may be unable to convict the perpetrator in court." The officer wouldn't want to convict anyone but the person who committed the crime.

4. c. Answer **a** is an assumption that is not based on anything written in the passage. Answer **b** is too specific—it is only one example of what happens to an officer who doesn't follow proper procedure. Not all cases of not following proper procedure could cost an officer his or her life. Only **c** is general enough to encompass the whole paragraph.

5. True. This sentence expresses the main idea.

6. True. This sentence is an opinion; it is debatable. Someone else might think that it is more important for a firefighter to follow proper procedure;

someone else might say it's more important for a construction worker to follow proper procedure. This is clearly what the writer thinks, not an established fact.

How did you do? If you got all six answers correct, congratulations! If you missed one or more questions, check the table below to see which lessons to review.

If you missed:	Then study:
Question 1	Lesson 2
Question 2	Lesson 1
Question 3	Lesson 3
Question 4	Lesson 2
Question 5	Lesson 2
Question 6	Lesson 4

PRACTICE PASSAGE 2

Try one more paragraph to conclude this first section. Once again, mark up the paragraph carefully and then answer the questions that follow.

Almost half of all Americans do not have health-care coverage. Those who do have coverage often pay exorbitant rates for their insurance. A young, healthy married couple in New York City, for example, must pay $359 per month to have only basic coverage from U.S. Healthcare; that coverage does not include eye care or dental care. Furthermore, this couple can only use U.S. Healthcare doctors. Most other HMOs (Health Maintenance Organizations) have similar programs that charge hard-working citizens outrageous fees for limited services. Even the most basic Medicare coverage through Blue Cross/Blue Shield costs a single adult over $600 a year—and this plan includes hundreds of dollars in deductibles. Americans need more adequate and affordable health-care coverage.

7. According to the passage, how many Americans have health-care coverage?
   a. all
   b. about one-third
   c. about one-half

8. A married couple in New York City must pay $359 to U.S. Healthcare
   a. each week
   b. each month
   c. each year

9. True or False: The U.S. Healthcare plan described does not include dental care.

10. U.S. Healthcare's plan allows patients to choose
   a. any doctor they wish
   b. any HMO doctor they wish
   c. among U.S. Healthcare doctors only

11. *Exorbitant* means
   a. extremely small
   b. excessive, unreasonable
   c. reasonable, appropriate

12. The main idea of this paragraph is best expressed in which sentence in the paragraph?

13. Indicate whether the following sentences are *fact* or *opinion*:
   a. "Those who do have coverage often pay exorbitant rates for their insurance."
   b. "Furthermore, this couple can only use U.S. Healthcare doctors."
   c. "Americans need more adequate and affordable health-care coverage."

Answers

7. c. See the first sentence.

8. b. See the third sentence.

9. True. See the third sentence.

10. c. See the fourth sentence.

11. b. There are several context clues. One is the use of the term *outrageous* in the fifth sentence to describe the health-care fees. Also, the last sentence complains that health care is not "affordable." Furthermore, the example the writer gives immediately after using the term *exorbitant*—$359 a month—shows that this word cannot mean **a**, *small*, and the use of the word *outrageous* shows that **c**, *reasonable*, cannot be the correct answer.

12. The last sentence. The point of the whole passage is that "Americans need more adequate and affordable health-care coverage."

13. Choice **a** is **opinion**. It is debatable whether the fees are exorbitant.
   Choice **b** is **fact**. This is verifiable information.
   Choice **c** is **opinion**. This is a debatable proposition.

How did you do this time? Better? If you missed any questions, this time *you* figure out which questions correspond with which lessons. This will help you see what categories you most need help with.

Skill Building Until Next Time

- Review the Skill Building sections from each lesson this week. Try any Skill Builders you didn't already do.
- Write a paragraph about what you've learned in this section. Begin your paragraph with a clear topic sentence, like: "I've learned several reading strategies since Lesson 1" or "I've learned that reading comprehension isn't as difficult as I thought." Then, write several sentences that support or explain your assertion. Try to use at least one vocabulary word that you've learned in this section.

STRUCTURE

ow that you've covered the basics, you can begin to focus on one specific reading comprehension strategy: structure. How do writers organize their ideas?

You might want to think of a writer as an architect. Every building has a number of rooms. But how these rooms are arranged is up to the architect. The same goes for a piece of writing—how the sentences and ideas are arranged is entirely up to the writer. However, most architects—and most writers—generally follow certain patterns, not because they can't think on their own, but because these patterns work. In this section, you'll study four organizational patterns that work for writers:

- Chronological order
- Order of importance
- Compare and contrast
- Cause and effect

You'll learn to recognize these patterns and some of the reasons why writers use them.

L·E·S·S·O·N 6

START FROM THE BEGINNING: CHRONOLOGICAL ORDER

LESSON SUMMARY

This lesson focuses on one of the simplest structures writers use: chronological order, or arrangement of events by the order in which they occured.

There are many ways to tell a story. Some stories start in the middle and flash backward to the beginning; a few start at the end and tell the story in reverse. But most of the time, stories start at the beginning. Writers often begin with what happened first and then tell what happened next, and next, and so on until the end. When writers tell a story in this order, from beginning to end in the order in which things happened, they are telling it in *chronological* order. *Chronology* is the arrangement of events in the order in which they occurred.

CHRONOLOGY AND TRANSITIONS

Much of what you read is arranged in chronological order. Newspaper and magazine articles, minutes of meetings, explanations of procedures, and so on are usually arranged this way. For example, look at the following paragraph that might be found in a company newsletter:

> This year's employee award ceremony was a tremendous success. The first award was given to Carlos Fe for Perfect Attendance. The second award, for Most Dedicated Employee, went to Jennifer Steele. Then our president, Martin Lucas, interrupted the awards ceremony to announce that he and his wife were having a baby. When he finished, everyone stood up for a congratulatory toast. Afterward, the third award was given to Karen Hunt for Most Inspiring Employee. Finally, President Lucas ended the ceremony by giving everyone a bonus check for $100.

You'll notice that this paragraph tells what happened at the ceremony from start to finish. You'll also notice that you can tell the order in which things happened in two ways. First, you can tell by the order of the sentences themselves—first things first, last things last. Second, you can tell by the use of *transitional words and phrases*, which signal a shift from one idea to the next. Here is the same paragraph with the transitional words underlined:

> This year's employee award ceremony was a tremendous success. The <u>first</u> award was given to Carlos Fe for Perfect Attendance. The <u>second</u> award, for Most Dedicated Employee, went to Jennifer Steele. <u>Then</u> the president, Martin Lucas, interrupted the awards ceremony to announce that he and his wife were having a baby. <u>When</u> he finished, everyone stood up for a congratulatory toast. <u>Afterward</u>, the <u>third</u> award was given to Karen Hunt for Most Inspiring Employee. <u>Finally</u>, President Lucas ended the ceremony by giving everyone a bonus check for $100.

The underlined words—*first, second, then, when, afterward, third*, and *finally*—are transitional words that keep these events linked together in chronological order. Look at how the paragraph sounds without these words:

> This year's employee award ceremony was a tremendous success. The award was given to Carlos Fe for Perfect Attendance. The award for Most Dedicated Employee went to Jennifer Steele. The president, Martin Lucas, interrupted the awards ceremony to announce that he and his wife were having a baby. He finished; everyone stood up for a congratulatory toast. The award was given to Karen Hunt for Most Inspiring Employee. President Lucas ended the ceremony by giving everyone a bonus check for $100.

It doesn't sound quite as good, does it?

PRACTICE WITH TRANSITIONAL WORDS AND PHRASES

PRACTICE PASSAGE 1

Here's a more extreme example of a paragraph with the transitional words and phrases omitted:

> I went to work early to get some extra filing done. I got there; the phone started ringing. My boss walked in. He asked me to type up a letter for him. He asked me to make arrangements for a client to stay in town overnight. I looked at my watch; it was already 11 o'clock.

Now, take the paragraph and add the following transitional words and phrases:

immediately	yesterday
as soon as	a moment later
when	then

_____ I went to work early to get some extra filing done. _____ I got there, the phone started ringing. _____ my boss walked in. _____ he asked me to type up a letter for him. _____ he asked me to make arrangements for a client to stay in town overnight. _____ I looked at my watch, it was already 11 o'clock.

See how much better the paragraph sounds with transitional words and phrases to guide you?

Answers

You might have come up with a slightly different version, but here's one good way to fill in the blanks:

Yesterday I went to work early to get some extra filing done. As soon as I got there, the phone started ringing. A moment later my boss walked in. Immediately he asked me to type up a letter for him. Then he asked me to make arrangements for a client to stay in town overnight. When I looked at my watch, it was already 11 o'clock.

PRACTICE PASSAGE 2

Here is a series of events listed in random order. Use the transitional words and phrases in each sentence to help you put them in proper chronological order. Number the sentences from 1–6 in the blank provided.

_____ *Once* the investigation is complete, you will be ranked.

_____ If you pass the exam, you must *then* have an oral interview.

_____ In order to become a corrections officer in Texas, you must complete several steps.

_____ *After* your interview has been scored, your background will be investigated.

_____ *Finally*, after you are accepted, you must take 120 hours of classroom instruction.

_____ *First*, you must take a written examination.

Answers

You should have numbered the blanks in this order: 5, 3, 1, 4, 6, 2. Here's how the sentences look together in a paragraph:

In order to become a corrections officer in Texas, you must complete several steps. First, you must take a written examination. If you pass the exam, you must then have an oral interview. After your interview has been scored, your background will be investigated. Once the investigation is complete, you will be ranked. Finally, after you are accepted, you must take 120 hours of classroom instruction.

PRACTICE PASSAGE 3

Remember the story of Mr. Blank, who came home to find that his apartment had been robbed? On the next page is the way his story was presented in Lesson 1.

On Tuesday, August 30, Mr. Blank, a prominent local citizen, arrived home from work to find his apartment had been robbed. The thieves somehow managed to slip past building security at 131 West Elm Street with nearly all of Mr. Blank's belongings. In fact, the thieves left behind nothing but a stack of old *Home Decorator* magazines and a can of pork and beans. The robbery was reported by Mr. Blank's neighbor, who found Mr. Blank unconscious in his doorway. Apparently Mr. Blank was so shocked by the robbery that he fainted. His neighbor immediately called an ambulance and then the police. Mr. Blank is now staying with relatives and is offering a reward of $25,000 for any information leading to the arrest of the thieves.

Notice that this paragraph is *not* arranged in chronological order. Take the ten different events that make up the story and rearrange them so that they are in chronological order.

Here's the order of events as they are presented in the story:

- Mr. Blank came home.
- His apartment was robbed.
- Thieves slipped by building security with his things.
- Thieves left only magazines and a can of pork and beans behind.
- Mr. Blank's neighbor reported the robbery.
- Mr. Blank was found by his neighbor.
- Mr. Blank fainted.
- Mr. Blank's neighbor called an ambulance.
- Mr. Blank's neighbor called the police.
- Mr. Blank offered a reward.

Now put the events in chronological order.

1.

2.

3.

4.

5.

6.

7.

8.

9.

10.

Now, take these chronologically ordered events and make them into a cohesive paragraph. To do this, you need to add transitional words and phrases. Here is a list of transitional words and phrases often used in chronologically organized passages:

first	soon
second	after
third	before
next	during
now	while
then	meanwhile
when	in the meantime
as soon as	at last
immediately	eventually
suddenly	finally

Write your paragraph, putting the events in chronological order with transitional phrases, below or on a separate piece of paper.

Answers

There are, of course, many possible ways of using transitional words and phrases to put Mr. Blank's story in chronological order. One paragraph might look like this:

> On Tuesday, Mr. Blank's apartment was robbed by thieves who slipped past building security with almost all Mr. Blank's things while Mr. Blank was at work. The thieves left only some magazines and a can of pork and beans behind. When Mr. Blank came home, he was so upset that he fainted. Soon Mr. Blank was found by his neighbor. His neighbor immediately called an ambulance and then called the police to report the robbery. Mr. Blank is now offering a $25,000 reward.

PRACTICE PASSAGE 4

Chronological order is very important, especially when it comes to procedures. If you perform the steps out of chronological order, you won't get the results you desire. Just imagine, for example, that you are trying to bake a cake. What happens when you do things out of order? You go without dessert.

Of course, the consequences of not following proper chronological order at work can be much more serious, so it's important that you strengthen this skill. Read the following paragraph, marking it up to help you keep track of the steps that an employee must follow in order to get tuition reimbursement.

Our company will be happy to reimburse you for college courses that enhance your job performance. Before you register for the course, you must get approval first from your immediate supervisor and then from Human Resources. If you are taking the course for credit, you must receive a C+ or better in the course. If you are not taking it for credit, you must pass the course. After you have completed the course, you must write a report explaining the content of the course and its relevance to your position. Then, you must fill out a reimbursement request. Attach a tuition payment receipt, your report, and a copy of your grades to this request and promptly submit this request to your supervisor. Once your supervisor has approved the request, you can then submit all of these forms to Human Resources, and you should receive your check within two weeks.

There are eight separate steps an employee must take in order to be reimbursed for college course work. What are they? List them below in the order in which the employee must do them.

1.

2.

3.

4.

5.

6.

7.

8.

If you marked up your paragraph, you should easily see the different steps. Here's how you might have marked it up. The transitional words and phrases are highlighted in bold.

> *need approval before registering!*
>
> Our company will be happy to reimburse you for college courses that enhance your job performance. (Before you register) for the course, you must get
> 1 + 2   approval **first** from your immediate supervisor and **then** from Human Resources.
> 3   If you are taking the course for credit, you must receive a C+ or better in the course. If you are not taking it for credit, you must pass the course. **After** you
> 4   have completed the course, you must write a report explaining the content of the course and its relevance to your position. **Then**, you must fill out a reim-
> 5 + 6   bursement request. Attach a tuition payment receipt, your report, and a copy of
> 7   your grades to this request and **promptly** submit this request to your supervisor. **Once** your supervisor has approved the request, you can **then** submit all of
> 8   these forms to Human Resources, and you should receive your check within two weeks.
>
> 1st – get supervisor approval
> 2nd – get HR approval
> 3rd – take course – get C+ or better!
> 4th – write report
> 5th – fill out reimb. request
> 6th – attach tuition, report + grades to request
> 7th – submit to supervisor
> 8th – submit to HR

If you miss a step in this process, you won't be reimbursed. Thus, it's critical that you be able to identify each step and the order in which the steps must be taken.

SUMMARY

Chronological structure is, of course, a very useful organizational pattern. Events happen in a certain order, so writers often present them in that order. Keep an eye out for the transitional words and phrases that signal this type of organization.

Skill Building Until Next Time

- As you think about things today, try to organize them chronologically. If you think back to something that happened to you over the weekend, for example, think about it in the order it happened: First I ____, then _____, suddenly, _____, and so on.
- As you read about events in the newspaper or in other places, put the different pieces of each event in chronological order, as you did with the story about Mr. Blank.

L·E·S·S·O·N 7
ORDER OF IMPORTANCE

LESSON SUMMARY

Continuing your study of the structure of reading material, this lesson shows you how writers use order of importance—from least to most important or from most to least important. Understanding this commonly used structure improves your reading comprehension by helping you see what's most important in a piece of writing.

t's a scientifically proven fact: People remember most what they learn *first* and *last* in a given session. Writers have instinctively known this for a long time. That's why many pieces of writing are organized not in chronological order but *by order of importance*.

Imagine again that the writer is like an architect. How would this type of writer arrange the rooms? By hierarchy. A *hierarchy* is a group of things arranged by rank or order of importance. In this type of organizational pattern, *hierarchy*, not chronology, determines order. Thus, this architect would lay the rooms out like so: When you walk in the front door, the first room you encounter would be the president's office, then the vice president's, then the assistant vice president's, and so on down to the lowest ranking worker. Or, vice versa, the architect may choose for you to meet the least important employee first, the one who has the least power in the company. Then the next, and the next, until at last you reach the president.

Likewise, in writing, ideas may be arranged in order of importance. In this pattern, which idea comes first? Not the one that *happened* first, but the one that is *most*, or *least*, important.

MOST IMPORTANT TO LEAST IMPORTANT

In the following paragraph, the writer starts with what is most important, hoping that by putting this item first, the reader will be sure to remember it. After you read the passage, answer the questions that follow. Each question is followed by its answer to guide you through your reading of the passage.

There are many things you can do to make tax time easier. The single most important thing you can do is to keep accurate records. Keep all of your pay stubs, receipts, bank statements, and so forth in a neat, organized folder so that when you're ready to prepare your form, all of your paperwork is in one place. The second thing you can do is start early. Get your tax forms from the post office as soon as they are available and start calculating. This way, if you run into any problems, you have plenty of time to straighten them out. You can also save time by reading the directions carefully. This will prevent time-consuming errors. Finally, if your taxes are relatively simple (you don't have any itemized deductions or special investments), use the shorter tax form. It's only one page, and if your records are in order, it can be completed in an hour or less.

1. According to the passage, what's the most important thing you can do to make tax time easier?

The answer, of course, should be clear: the writer tells you clearly that the "single most important thing" is to "keep accurate records."

2. What is the second most important thing you can do to make tax time easier?

When a writer starts out by saying "the most important thing," you know that the writer will be starting with the most important idea and ending with the least important. The second best thing, therefore, is the second piece of advice offered in the paragraph: "start early."

3. What's the third most important thing?

Did you write "Read the directions carefully"? Good.

4. Finally, what is the *least* important tip the writer offers?

Of course, the answer is the last piece of advice the writer offers: Use the short form if you can.

LEAST IMPORTANT TO MOST IMPORTANT

Some writers prefer the opposite approach, depending on the subject and the effect they want their writing to have. Rather than *starting* with the most important idea, they prefer to *end* with what is most important. Not only do they leave you with a strong concluding impression, but they also take advantage of the "snowball effect." The snowball effect is the "build up" or force that a writer gets from starting with what's least important and moving toward what's most important. Like a snowball, the writer's idea builds and builds, gets bigger and bigger, more and more important. By starting with the least important point, writers can also create suspense—the reader is waiting for that final idea. And each idea or item builds upon the ones that come before it (as in a snowball).

Here's an example of a paragraph that builds from least important to most important. Read the paragraph, marking it up as you go along. Answer the questions that follow.

There are a number of reasons why there should not be dress-down days at work. First of all, workplaces need to maintain a conscious distinction between the professional and the casual. This distinction is maintained largely by dress. When this distinction vanishes, workers might begin to be more casual with each other, making it difficult to maintain a professional atmosphere.

More importantly, casual wear destroys company hierarchy. When the president of the company comes to work wearing khaki pants and a polo shirt, employees are likely to say, "Why, he's just one of us." While in "real life" he may indeed be their equal, in the workplace he is not.

But the most important reason employees should not be allowed to come to work dressed casually is because it drastically decreases productivity. When people are dressed in their work clothes, they work; when they are dressed casually, the temptation to be casual about getting work done is too great. Employees spend a great deal of time milling about and have a great tendency to cut corners: "Oh, I don't need to proofread this again. It's good enough." This attitude in the workplace can not only be dangerous to a company's welfare—it can be deadly.

In the spaces below, first list the reasons the author provides for being against dressing casually at work *in the order in which they are listed in the passage.* In the next set of blanks, list those same reasons *in their order of importance.*

Order of Presentation

1.

2.

3.

Order of Importance

1.

2.

3.

You see, of course, that the orders are reversed: The author starts with what is least important and ends with what is most important. Why? Why not the other way around?

This author uses a least-to-most-important organizational strategy because he is making an argument. He's trying to convince you that it's not a good idea to have dress-down days at work. In order to be convincing, he must have a pretty strong argument. If he starts with what he feels is his most important (and most convincing) point, he has already shown his hand, so to speak. And he hasn't "warmed you up" yet. Especially when the issue is controversial, writers often use the least-to-most-important structure. That way, if their less important points make sense to the reader, then their more important points will come off even stronger. Also, if they were to organize their ideas in the reverse order, most to least important, readers might feel let down.

Thus, you can often expect to see this type of structure—least to most important—in an argument. As the saying goes, "save the best for last." In an argument, that's usually where "the best" has the most impact.

In the first example, about preparing for tax time, the writer was not trying to convince. She was simply giving some advice. There's no need, then, for a build-up. Indeed, in that kind of paragraph, the reader might stop reading after the first tip if he or she doesn't find it helpful. That's why the most important ideas come first—to make sure they'll be read.

In other words, the writer's *purpose*, his or her motive for writing, influences the choice of organizational patterns. In turn, the structure influences how you take in and understand what you read.

PRACTICE

Look at the following list of reasons to read more often. If you were to put these reasons together in a paragraph to convince readers that they should read more, how would you organize them? Rank these reasons first in order of importance and then in the order in which you would present them.

Five Reasons to Read More Often

- It will improve your vocabulary.
- It will improve your reading comprehension.
- It will increase your reading speed.
- It will broaden your understanding of yourself and others.
- It will introduce you to new information and ideas.

Order of Importance to You

1.

2.

3.

4.

5.

Order of Presentation

1.

2.

3.

4.

5.

In which order did you choose to present your ideas? Most important to least important? Or least to most? Either structure will work beautifully with these ideas. You may want to hit your readers with what's most important from the start so that you make sure you catch their attention. Or you may want to save your best idea for last so that your readers get through all the other ideas first and build up to the most important. You might present the ideas differently, but below are two versions of the resulting paragraph as examples.

Example: Most to Least Important

There are many benefits to reading more often. First and foremost, reading more will broaden your understanding of yourself and of other people. It will also introduce you to new information and ideas. Furthermore, it will improve your overall reading comprehension so you'll begin to understand more of what you read. In addition, reading more will improve your vocabulary and increase your reading speed.

Example: Least to Most Important

There are many benefits to reading more often. First of all, it will increase your reading speed, so that you can read more in less time. Second, it will improve your vocabulary. Third, it will improve your overall reading comprehension, and you'll understand more of what you read. In addition, reading more will introduce you to new information and ideas. Most importantly, it will broaden your understanding of yourself and of other people.

REVIEW
Transitions

Notice how the transitional words and phrases are used in the paragraphs above. Go back to each paragraph and underline the transitional words and phrases.

Here are the words you should have underlined in the first paragraph: *first and foremost, also, furthermore, in addition.* The second paragraph uses different transitional words and phrases: *first of all, second, third, in addition,* and *most importantly.*

Main Idea

By the way, what is the main idea of the two paragraphs above? Do you see a topic sentence? Write the main idea of the paragraphs in the space below.

You can probably recognize by now that the first sentence in each paragraph, "There are many benefits to reading more often," is the topic sentence that governs each paragraph. This sentence is general enough to encompass each of the different reasons given, and it makes an assertion about reading—that you should do it more often.

SUMMARY

Organizing ideas by order of importance is a structure you will see often. Whether a passage is organized from most to least important or least to most, this technique should now be easy for you to recognize.

Skill Building Until Next Time

- As you come across lists today, see how they are organized. Are they organized by order of importance? If so, are the items listed from least to most important or from most to least? If the lists are not organized hierarchically, try to organize them by their order of importance.
- Create your own "order of importance" paragraphs like the one on reasons to read more often. Some topics you might write about are reasons for a four-day work week, reasons why yours is the best career, things you need to get done this week, and so forth.

L·E·S·S·O·N 8

SIMILARITIES AND DIFFERENCES: COMPARE AND CONTRAST

LESSON SUMMARY

Today's lesson explores another organizational pattern writers often use to structure their writing: comparison and contrast.

e spend a good deal of our lives comparing and contrasting things. Whenever we want to explain something, for example, we often use *comparison* (showing how two or more things are *similar*). We might say, for example, that mint chocolate chip ice cream tastes just like a York Peppermint Pattie; or that the new manager looks just like Clint Eastwood. When we want to show how things are *different* or not alike, we *contrast* them. We might say that York Peppermint Patties are mintier than any mint chocolate chip ice cream; or that the new manager may look like Eastwood, but he doesn't have Eastwood's dimple.

How Comparison and Contrast Work

What writers do when they compare and contrast is provide a way of classifying or judging the items they're analyzing. They show how two (or more) things are similar or different when placed side by side. Consider, for example, the following paragraph. Read it carefully and then answer the questions that follow. The answers are after the questions.

Planting a garden is a lot like having a family. Both require a great deal of work, especially as they grow and as the seasons change. As summer days lengthen, your plants become dependent on you for sustenance much like your children depend on you for food and drink. Like a thirsty child asking for a drink of water, your plants do the same. Their bent, wilted "body" language, translated, issues a demand much the way your child requests milk or juice. When their collective thirsts are quenched, you see the way both of them thrive in your care. The fussy child becomes satisfied, and the plant reaches toward the sun in a showy display. You might also find that you have to neaten up and tidy the space around your plants much like you would pick up toys and clothes that have been thrown helter-skelter in your toddler's room. Similarly, plants shed spent petals, roses need to be pruned, and weeds need to be pulled. To keep children healthy, parents protect their children against disease with medicine, and gardeners do the same with insect repellent. To nourish them, parents give children vitamins, and gardeners use fertilizer as both promote healthy growth. As children grow and become adults, they need less and less care. However, here's where the similarity ends. While plants die and become dormant during winter, children still maintain a vital role in the family unit.

FINDING THE FACTS

1. What two things are being compared and contrasted here?

2. In what ways are these two things similar? (There are four similarities; list them below.)
   a.

   b.

   c.

   d.

3. In what ways are these two things different? (There is one aspect that is different; write it below.)

Answers

1. The two things being compared and contrasted are a parent and a gardener.
2. Gardeners are like parents in that: a) plants are dependent on gardeners as children are on parents; b) plants require care from gardeners as children do from their parents; c) gardeners tidy up after their plants, as parents do after children; and d) gardeners protect their plants, as parents protect their children.
3. Gardeners are unlike parents in that their responsibility for their plants ends when the plant dies or goes into winter dormancy.

FINDING THE MAIN IDEA

Now that you've answered those questions, consider one more. Look at the passage above again, and then answer this question:

4. What is the main idea of this passage?

Did you notice that the opening sentence, "Planting a garden is a lot like having a family," is the topic sentence that expresses the main idea of this paragraph? The paragraph does mention a *difference* between these two roles, but notice that the topic sentence does not claim that gardeners and parents are *exactly* alike. Instead, it asserts that they are "a lot" alike.

TRANSITIONAL DEVICES

As you read the paragraph about gardeners and parents, did you notice the transitional words and phrases that show you when the writer is comparing (showing similarity) and when the writer is contrasting (showing difference)? Here's the passage once more. As you read it this time, underline the transitional words and phrases you find.

Planting a garden is a lot like having a family. Both require a great deal of work, especially as they grow and as the seasons change. As summer days lengthen, your plants become dependent on you for sustenance much like your children depend on you for food and drink. Like a thirsty child asking for a drink of water, your plants do the same. Their bent, wilted "body" language, translated, issues a demand much the way your child requests milk or juice. When their collective thirsts are quenched, you see the way both of them thrive in your care. The fussy child becomes satisfied, and the plant reaches toward the sun in a showy display. You might also find that you have to neaten up and tidy the space

around your plants much like you would pick up toys and clothes that have been thrown helter-skelter in your toddler's room. Similarly, plants shed spent petals, roses need to be pruned, and weeds need to be pulled. To keep children healthy, parents protect their children against disease with medicine, and gardeners do the same with insect repellent. To nourish them, parents give children vitamins, and gardeners use fertilizer as both promote healthy growth. As children grow and become adults, they need less and less care. However, here's where the similarity ends. While plants die and become dormant during winter, children still maintain a vital role in the family unit.

There are several transitional words and phrases writers use to show comparison and contrast. In this paragraph, you should have underlined the following words: *much like, in the same way, similarly,* and *however.* Below is a more complete list of transitional words and phrases.

Here are some words and phrases that show similarity:

similarly	in the same way
likewise	in a like manner
like	and
just as	also

These are words and phrases that show difference:

but	yet
on the other hand	on the contrary
however	nevertheless
conversely	

STRUCTURE

Now look more closely at the sample paragraph to examine its structure. Exactly how is this paragraph organized?

First, you've noticed that the paragraph begins with a topic sentence that makes the initial comparison:

gardeners are like parents. Then, the paragraph identifies four ways in which gardeners are like parents:

1. Plants become dependent upon gardeners as children do on parents.

2. Plants require care from their gardeners as children do from parents.

3. Gardeners tidy up after their plants as parents do after children.

4. Gardeners protect plants from "dangers" as parents protect children.

Finally, after pointing out these similarities, the paragraph concludes by pointing out an important difference between parents and gardeners:

1. A gardener's responsibility for his or her plants ends with time while a parent's doesn't.

Perhaps you noticed something else in the way this paragraph is organized. Did you notice that every time the paragraph mentions something about a parent's role, it also mentions something about a gardener? Each aspect of the gardener's role that is discussed is followed by a comparable aspect of the parent's role. Thus, for every aspect of "A" (the gardener), the paragraph provides a comparable aspect of "B" (the parent) to compare or contrast. The paragraph is therefore organized like this: ABABABABAB.

This is called the **point-by-point** method of comparison and contrast. Each aspect of A that is discussed is immediately paired with that aspect of B (being dependent, requiring care, cleaning up, and protecting).

On the other hand, some writers prefer to deal first with all aspects of A and then with all aspects of B. This is called the **block** method of comparison and contrast;

it goes AAAAABBBBB. Here is the same paragraph arranged using the block method:

Planting a garden is a lot like having a family. A plant becomes dependent on the gardener and begs for water on a hot summer day. Gardeners also have to tidy up the space around their plants as they shed spent petals, as they require pruning, and as they become choked with weeds. Gardeners also provide for the health of their plants through insecticide and fertilizer applications. A gardener's responsibility for his or her plants lessens as they die at the end of the season or they go into winter dormancy.

Like a gardener, a parent finds their children dependent upon them for food and nourishment. Like a gardener, a parent is constantly picking up after their children, as toys and clothes are scattered throughout the house. Like a gardener, a parent provides for the nourishment and well-being of their children with vitamin supplements, food, and medicines. However, unlike gardeners, parents will find that their responsibility lessens as the child grows, but it does not come to an end.

Here, the passage treats each of the things being compared and contrasted separately—first, all aspects of the gardener, then all aspects of the parent—rather than one aspect of the gardener, one of the parent; another of the gardener, another of the parent. So the organization is quite different.

But you should notice one thing that is the same in both passages: They compare and contrast aspects of A and B that are comparable or parallel. When an aspect of A is discussed, that same aspect of B (whether it is similar to or different from A) must be discussed. This correspondence of parts is essential for the compare and contrast technique. Look what happens, for example, when the writer does not discuss corre-sponding parts:

> Being a parent is a lot like being a gardener. Parents must bathe, clothe, and feed their children. Parents must also create and maintain guidelines for acceptable behavior for children. Also, parents must see to it that their children get a proper education.
>
> Gardeners nurture the plants in their gardens. They pull weeds and prune them to encourage them to grow. They feed them and apply insecticides. They watch them flower and then witness their demise.

You'll notice that this passage seems to focus on differences between gardeners and parents rather than the similarities. But is this really a fair contrast? Look at the aspects of A (the gardener) that are described here. Do they have any relationship to the aspects of B (the parent) that are described? No. And a compare and contrast passage can't be successful unless the aspects of A and B are discussed comparably. The two paragraphs above don't really seem to have a point—there's no basis for comparison between gardeners and parents.

PRACTICE

Suppose you were going to write a paragraph that compares and contrasts readers and detectives. There are five aspects of being a reader and five aspects of being a detective listed below. Only *three* items in each list are comparable. Find those three items in each list and pair them with their matching item. Remember, these items may be either similarities or differences. What's important is that they are comparable aspects.

A reader:

1. Looks for clues to meaning.
2. Has many different types of books to read.
3. Can choose what book to read.
4. Builds vocabulary by reading.
5. Becomes a better reader with each book.

A detective:

1. Has a dangerous job.
2. Gets better at solving crimes with each case.
3. Requires lots of training.
4. Doesn't get to choose which cases to work on.
5. Looks for clues to solve the crime.

Did you find the aspects that are comparable? Did you match Reader 1 with Detective 5 (similarity)? Reader 3 with Detective 4 (difference)? And Reader 5 with Detective 2 (similarity)? If so, you did terrific work.

Here's how this information might work together in a paragraph:

> In many ways, readers are a lot like detectives. Like detectives looking for clues at the scene of the crime, readers look for clues to meaning in the books that they read. And, like detectives who get better and better at solving crimes with each case, readers get better and better at understanding what they read with each book. Unfortunately for detectives, however, they cannot choose which cases they get to work on, whereas readers have the pleasure of choosing which books they'd like to read.

WHY COMPARE AND CONTRAST?

In addition to following the ABABAB or AAABBB structure, compare and contrast passages must, like all other passages, have a point. There's a reason that these two items are being compared and contrasted; there's something the writer is trying to point out by putting these two things side by side for analysis. This reason or point is the main idea, which is often stated in a topic sentence.

The main idea of the first paragraph you looked at in this lesson was, "Planting a garden is a lot like having a family." In this paragraph, you learned that the writer sees a significant similarity between these two roles. Likewise, in the paragraph above, you see a significant similarity between readers and detectives.

In both cases, you may never have thought of making such comparisons. That's part of the beauty of the compare and contrast organization: It often allows you to see things in a new and interesting way. In addition, it serves the more practical function of showing you how two things measure up against each other so that you can make informed decisions, like about which car to buy (a compare and contrast essay might tell you which car is better) or which savings bond to invest in (a compare and contrast essay will show you which bond is best for you).

Skill Building Until Next Time

- As you go through your day, compare and contrast things around you. Compare and contrast, for example, your current job to your previous one. How are they alike? How are they different? Make sure the aspects of the two things that you analyze are comparable. For example, you might want to compare and contrast the salaries, responsibilities, and benefits at both jobs.

- As you make these comparisons, or if you notice compare and contrast passages in what you read, practice arranging them in both point-by-point order (ABABAB) and in block order (AAABBB).

L · E · S · S · O · N 9

WHY DO THINGS HAPPEN? A LOOK AT CAUSE AND EFFECT

LESSON SUMMARY

"One thing leads to another"—that's the principle behind cause and effect. Understanding cause and effect, and the relationship between them, will make you a better reader.

For every action," the famous scientist Sir Isaac Newton said, "there is an equal and opposite reaction." Every action results in another action (a *re*action); or, for every action, there is an *effect* caused by that action. Likewise, each action is *caused* by a previous action. In other words, each action has a *cause*—something that made it happen—and each action has an *effect*—something it makes happen.

- **Cause:** a person or thing that makes something happen or produces an effect.
- **Effect:** a change produced by an action or cause.

Much of what you read is an attempt to explain either the cause of some action or its effect. For example, an author might try to explain the causes of World War I or the effect of underwater nuclear testing; the reason behind a change in policy at work or the effect a new computer system will have on office procedure. Let's take a look at how writers explaining cause or effect might organize their ideas.

DISTINGUISHING CAUSE FROM EFFECT

A passage that examines cause generally answers the question *why* something took place: Why was the company restructured? Who or what made this take place? A passage that examines effect generally answers the question *what happened* after something took place: What happened as a result of the restructuring? How did it affect the company?

PRACTICE

To help you distinguish between cause and effect, look carefully at the sentences below. You'll see that cause and effect work together; you can't have one without the other. That's why it's very important to be able to distinguish between the two. See if you can determine both the cause and the effect in each of the following sentences:

Example: Robin got demoted when he talked back to the boss.
Cause: Robin talked back to the boss.
Effect: Robin got demoted.

1. Inflation has caused us to raise our prices.
   Cause:

   Effect:

2. Since we hired Joan, the office has been running smoothly.
   Cause:

   Effect:

3. He realized that his car had stopped not because it needed repair but because it ran out of gas.
   Cause:

   Effect:

4. The company's budget crisis was created by overspending.
   Cause:

   Effect:

5. As a result of our new marketing program, sales have doubled.
   Cause:

   Effect:

Answers

1. Cause: *Inflation*
   Effect: *We had to raise our prices.*
2. Cause: *We hired Joan.*
   Effect: *Our office has been running smoothly.*
3. Cause: *The car ran out of gas.*
   Effect: *The car stopped.*
4. Cause: *Overspending*
   Effect: *Budget crisis*
5. Cause: *The new marketing program*
   Effect: *Sales have doubled.*

You were probably guided in your answers to the exercise above by the words and phrases that indicate when a cause or effect is being examined. Below is a partial list of such words.

Words Indicating Cause

because (of)	created (by)
since	caused (by)

Words Indicating Effect

since	therefore
hence	consequently
so	as a result

WHEN CAUSE AND EFFECT ARE INTERRELATED

Notice how the signal words listed on the previous page are used in the following paragraph. Underline the signal words as you come across them.

Ed became a mechanic largely because of his father. His father was always in the garage working on one car or another, so young Ed would spend hours watching his father work. As a result, he became fascinated by cars at an early age. His father encouraged him to learn about cars on his own, so Ed began tinkering with cars himself at age eight. Consequently, by the time he was 13, Ed could tear an engine apart and put it back together by himself. Since he was already so skilled, when he was 15 he got a job as the chief mechanic at a local repair shop. He has been there ever since.

You should have underlined the following signal words and phrases in the paragraph above: *because of, so* (twice), *as a result, consequently,* and *since.*

Notice that this paragraph's purpose—to explain *why* Ed became a mechanic—is expressed in the topic sentence, "Ed became a mechanic largely because of his father." This paragraph's purpose, then, is to explain cause, and the primary cause is Ed's father.

You'll notice, however, that some of the sentences in this paragraph also deal with effect. This may seem like a contradiction at first. After all, why would a paragraph about cause deal with effect? But it's not a contradiction. That's because there isn't just *one* thing that led to Ed's becoming a mechanic. Although Ed's dad may have been the initial cause, there was still a *series* of actions and reactions that took place—a series of causes and effects. Once A causes B, B then becomes the cause for C.

In fact, there are six different sets of cause and effect listed in this paragraph. What are they? The first cause is provided to get you started.

Cause 1: Ed's father was always in the garage.

Effect 1:

Cause 2:

Effect 2:

Cause 3:

Effect 3:

Cause 4:

Effect 4:

Cause 5:

Effect 5:

Cause 6:

Effect 6:

Answers

Cause 1: Ed's father was always in the garage.
Effect 1: Ed would spend hours watching.

Cause 2: Ed would spend hours watching.
Effect 2: Ed became fascinated by cars.

Cause 3: Ed became fascinated by cars.
Effect 3: Ed began tinkering with cars.

Cause 4: Ed began tinkering with cars.
Effect 4: Ed's father encouraged him.

Cause 5: Ed's father encouraged him.
Effect 5: Ed could tear an engine apart by himself.

Cause 6: Ed could tear an engine apart by himself.
Effect 6: He got a job as the chief mechanic.

VARIATIONS

WHEN ONE CAUSE HAS SEVERAL EFFECTS

Sometimes one cause may have several effects: Several things may happen as a result of one action. In the passage below, the writer explains several effects of the new marketing campaign:

Our new marketing campaign has been a tremendous success. Since we've been advertising on the radio, sales have increased by 35 percent. Our client references have doubled, and we've had greater client retention rates. Furthermore, we've been able to hire five new sales representatives and expand our territory to include the southwestern United States.

According to the paragraph above, what have been the effects of the new marketing campaign?

1.

2.

3.

4.

5.

Answers

1. Sales have increased 35 percent.
2. Client references have doubled.
3. Client retention rates have increased.
4. Five new sales representatives have been hired.
5. Territory has been expanded to include the Southwest.

WHEN ONE EFFECT HAS SEVERAL CAUSES

Just as one action can have many results, one action can have many causes as well. The following memo is an example.

TO: Joe Smith
FROM: Management

This memorandum is to clarify the circumstances of your dismissal. Although you may think we've dismissed you because of your recent absenteeism, there are, in fact, several reasons behind our decision to terminate you. In addition to your excessive absence, you have failed to complete your monthly and weekly reports in a timely manner. In fact, many times we've received them so late that we were unable to include your figures in our budget reports. Furthermore, we have had several complaints recently regarding your conduct in the office, and several supervisors have reported your refusal to follow our company dress code. While none of these offenses would be worthy of dismissal on an individual basis, combined they leave us no choice but to terminate your employment.

Why did Joe Smith get fired? List the causes below:

1.

2.

3.

4.

Answers

You should have noticed that there were four causes:

1. Joe's excessive absenteeism.
2. Joe's late reports.
3. Complaints about Joe's conduct.
4. Joe's refusal to follow the dress code.

CONTRIBUTING VS. SUFFICIENT CAUSE

You'll notice that the memorandum above tells Mr. Smith that "none of these offenses would be worthy of dismissal on an individual basis." This means that each of these causes is a **contributing** cause. A *contributing* cause is one that *helps* to make something happen but can't make that thing happen by itself. It is only one factor that *contributes* to the cause.

On the opposite end of the cause spectrum is the **sufficient** cause. A *sufficient* cause is an event that, by itself, is strong enough to make the event happen. Sufficient cause is demonstrated in the following paragraph.

Dear Mr. X:

We have recently learned that you have breached our Confidentiality Agreement. When you joined our company, you agreed not to reveal any of our company secrets to the competition. You also agreed that if you were found in violation of this agreement, your employment would be terminated. Consequently, we hereby terminate your employment, effective immediately. Please see Myra in Payroll for your final paycheck.

Here, you can see that there is one clear reason why Mr. X is being fired: He breached the Confidentiality Agreement. (If you don't know what *breach* means, you should be able to determine the meaning from the context.)

EVALUATING OPINIONS ABOUT CAUSE AND EFFECT

Sometimes in a cause and effect passage, an author will offer his or her *opinion* about the cause or effect of something rather than *facts* about the cause or effect. In that case, readers must judge the validity of the author's analysis. Are the author's ideas logical? Does he or she support the conclusions he or she comes to? Consider, for example, two authors' opinions about how a no-smoking policy would affect their office.

Paragraph A

A no-smoking policy would be disastrous. Over one-third of our employees smoke an average of three-quarters of a pack each per day. Since they will no longer be allowed to smoke in the office, they will need to take longer breaks (since they must now leave the building in order to smoke). As a result, they will be less productive. In addition, because their breaks must be longer, they must take fewer breaks and only at certain times in the day when they are able to get away for longer periods of time. Consequently, there will be long stretches of time between cigarettes for them, so many of these employees will be extremely irritable. This irritability will inevitably affect their coworkers. Furthermore, many long-term smokers will simply quit their jobs rather than put up with this irritability. They will simply find another company that will let them smoke at work.

Paragraph B

A no-smoking policy will be a tremendous benefit to all of our employees. If smoking is eliminated in the office, all employees will be able to breathe air free from any second-hand smoke while at work. Furthermore, our clean air won't drive out any potential clients or employees who are irritated by smoke. In addition, those who do smoke may find it easier to quit or at least reduce the number of cigarettes they smoke during the day because cigarette breaks will not be as accessible. Also, employees will be more productive since they won't be able to take such frequent cigarette breaks. Finally, we will be able to reduce the cost of our health-care benefits once our office officially becomes a no-smoking environment. This will save every employee money.

What effects does Author A think a no-smoking policy would have?

1.

2.

3.

4.

5.

What effects does Author B think a no-smoking policy would have?

1.

2.

3.

4.

5.

You'll notice that both authors take one cause—a no-smoking policy—and offer several possible effects. Often, authors will use the cause-and-effect structure to make arguments like the ones we've just seen: one for and one against a no-smoking policy. It is up to the reader to determine whose argument seems most valid.

SUMMARY

Understanding cause and effect is an important skill not only for reading comprehension but also for your daily life. In order to analyze the events happening around you, you have to be able to understand *why* those events happened—what caused them. Similarly, in order to make decisions or evaluate the decisions of others, you need to be able to think about the effects of a possible decision. "Reading," not only texts but also events and situations, requires you to understand cause and effect.

Skill Building Until Next Time

- As you work today, consider the effects of any recent changes in your office, such as new equipment that's been installed, a new system or procedure that's been put in place, a new manager or other employee. How will these changes affect the work place? Your job in particular? Or forecast the effect of changes that are coming. For example, how will the upcoming layoffs affect the company?

- Consider recent events at home or at work. What might have caused them? For example, if a coworker just got a promotion, consider what he or she might have done to get that promotion. Or if a child is having trouble at school, what might be causing that trouble?

L · E · S · S · O · N

BEING STRUCTURALLY SOUND: PUTTING IT ALL TOGETHER

10

LESSON SUMMARY

Today's lesson pulls together what you've learned in Lessons 6–9 and gives you more practice in discerning the structure of a reading passage.

L ike an architect designing a building, a writer must have a blue-print—a plan for how he or she will organize the passage. So far in this section we've looked at several ways that authors may organize their information and ideas:

- **Lesson 6: Chronological order.** Ideas are arranged in the order in which they occurred (or in the order in which they should occur).

- **Lesson 7: Order of importance.** Ideas are arranged in order of *increasing* importance (least important idea to most important idea) or in order of *decreasing* importance (most important idea to least important idea).

- **Lesson 8: Compare and contrast.** Ideas are arranged so that parallel aspects of item A and item B are compared and contrasted either in block style (AAAABBBB) or point-by-point style (ABABABAB).

- **Lesson 9: Cause and effect.** Ideas are arranged so that readers can see what event or series of events *caused* something to take place or what *effect* an event or series of events had.

If any of the terms or strategies on the previous page seem unfamiliar to you, STOP. Please take a few moments to review whatever lesson is unclear.

PRACTICE

Although writers often rely on one particular structure to organize their ideas, in many cases, writers use a combination of these structures. For example, a writer may want to compare and contrast the causes of World War I and those of World War II; or a writer may want to describe, in chronological order, the events that led to (caused) the failure of the computer system. Thus, today we will look at how writers may combine these strategies. In addition, we'll continue to strengthen your reading comprehension skills by including strategies from the first week:

- Finding the facts
- Determining the main idea
- Defining vocabulary words in context
- Distinguishing between fact and opinion

PRACTICE PASSAGE 1

Begin with the following paragraph. Read it carefully, marking it up as you go. Then answer the questions that follow.

There are several reasons behind our decision to close the Florida office. The first difficulty occurred last May, when our long-time manager, John Doe, resigned. Although he left the company for purely personal reasons, and although sales were at their highest in months, many employees saw his departure as a symptom that the company was in trouble, and within a week after Mr. Doe's departure, several other employees quit. We were unable to fill Mr. Doe's position for some time, since all the candidates we interviewed were either discouraged by the number of employee vacancies or didn't have the experience to handle the work. Then the sales dropped dramatically, and, as a result, the office was unable to meet its monthly expenses. At the same time, our central office tightened its budget, so we lacked sufficient funds to revitalize the office. After a board meeting in August, we decided to close the office permanently. We will, of course, help relocate employees who wish to stay with the firm.

1. Which two organizational strategies does this writer use?
   a. chronological order
   b. order of importance
   c. compare and contrast
   d. cause and effect

2. *Revitalize* means
   a. to be very important, vital
   b. to relocate
   c. to bring back to life

3. What started the trouble in the Florida office?

4. What happened after the initial cause set things in motion?

a.

b.

c.

d.

e.

f.

Answers

1. **a, d.** The writer tells you the causes, in the order in which they occurred, that resulted in the closing of the Florida office.

2. **c.** You can tell from the context of the surrounding sentences that the company could not invest money in the office, and therefore the office had to be closed. If they could have invested money in the office, it is likely that they would have been able to bring the dying office back to life.

3. John Doe's resignation started the trouble in the Florida office.

4. After John Doe resigned, the following events occurred in this order:

a. The other employees quit.

b. They were unable to fill John Doe's position.

c. Sales dropped.

d. The office was unable to meet its expenses.

e. The central office tightened its budget.

f. They decided to close the office.

How did you do? Were you able to see how each cause led to an effect, and how that effect caused something else to happen (another effect)? If you missed any of the questions, here's what you should do:

If you missed:	Then study:
Question 1	Lessons 6 and 9
Question 2	Lesson 3
Question 3	Lesson 9
Question 4	Lesson 9

PRACTICE PASSAGE 2

Now try the passage on the next page. Again, read it carefully, marking it up as you go, and then answer the questions that follow.

There are several changes in the procedure for employees who wish to apply for vacant positions within the company. These changes make it much easier for in-house employees to fill vacancies that occur within the company.

First, the most important difference is that employees will now be notified of all available positions *before* the positions are advertised for the general public. Accordingly, all in-house candidates will be interviewed before we see any outside candidates, and we will offer the job to outside candidates only if no current employees are able to fill the position only.

Second, under the new procedure in-house employees can be hired even if they don't meet all job requirements. Under our old policy, in-house employees had to meet all job qualifications in order to obtain the vacant position. Now, however, employees who have proven themselves dedicated to the company will be hired for a vacant position even if they are lacking some minor qualifications; training will be provided.

A third change involves recommendations. From now on, employees do not need to be recommended for an in-house position before they apply. Instead, employees may apply as soon as they are aware of the vacancy. The remaining procedures and policies (those regarding increase in pay, interview procedure, and hiring approval) remain the same.

5. Which two organizational strategies does this writer use?
   a. chronological order
   b. order of importance
   c. compare and contrast
   d. cause and effect

6. The author organizes his ideas in order of
   a. decreasing importance (most important to least important)
   b. increasing importance (least important to most important)

7. Underline the sentence in this passage that expresses the main idea.

8. The sentence you underlined is
   a. fact
   b. opinion

Answers

5. b, c. The author uses order of importance in comparing the old procedure to the new one.

6. a. The author organizes his ideas in order of decreasing importance. He starts with the most important change ("First, the most important difference is . . .") and moves downward to the second and third most important changes.

7. The sentence that expresses the main idea of all four paragraphs is the second sentence in the first paragraph: "These changes make it much easier for in-house employees to fill vacancies." Although the first sentence tells us what all the paragraphs will be about (the changes in the procedure), it is the second sentence that expresses an opinion—how the author feels about this subject—and therefore it is the main idea.

8. b. This sentence expresses an opinion, not a fact. There have indeed been changes—that is a fact—but whether those changes make things easier for most employees is debatable. There may be some things about the old procedure that we don't know. Perhaps, for example, they opened the job to both in-house employees and the general public at the same time, but they interviewed all in-house employees first anyway. Because of our limited information about the old procedure, we cannot accept the idea that the change is better as fact.

If you missed some of these questions, now it's up to you to figure out which lessons to review.

PRACTICE PASSAGE 3

Now it's your turn. In this exercise, you'll take a paragraph that is organized one way—by cause and effect—and add another structure: order of importance.

Here's what you should do: Re-read the two passages about the effect of a no-smoking policy. Decide which author you agree with most. Then, look carefully at the effects the author predicts. Which effect do you think is most important? Which is least important? Rank these effects in order of importance. Then, decide whether you want to start with the most important idea and end with the least important, or, vice versa, start with the least important and end with the most important. Finally, put it all together in a paragraph in the space provided.

Paragraph A

A no-smoking policy would be disastrous. Over one-third of our employees smoke an average of three-quarters of a pack each per day. Since they will no longer be allowed to smoke in the office, they will need to take longer breaks (since they must now leave the building in order to smoke). As a result, they will be less productive. In addition, because their breaks must be longer, they must take fewer breaks and only at certain times in the day when they are able to get away for longer periods of time. Consequently, there will be long stretches of time between cigarettes for them, so many of these employees will be extremely irritable. This irritability will inevitably affect their coworkers. Furthermore, many long-term smokers will simply quit their jobs rather than put up with this irritability. They will simply find another company that will let them smoke at work.

Paragraph B

A no-smoking policy will be a tremendous benefit to all of our employees. If smoking is eliminated in the office, all employees will be able to breathe air free from any second-hand smoke while at work. Furthermore, our clean air won't drive out any potential clients or employees who are irritated by smoke. In addition, those who do smoke may find it easier to quit or at least reduce the number of cigarettes they smoke during the day because cigarette breaks will not be as accessible. Also, employees will be more productive since they won't be able to take such frequent cigarette breaks. Finally, we will be able to reduce the cost of our health-care benefits once our office officially becomes a no-smoking environment. This will save every employee money.

1. Rank the ideas of the paragraph you have chosen in order of their importance to you.

2. Now write a paragraph, choosing whether to put the ideas in the order of increasing importance or decreasing importance.

Skill Building Until Next Time

- Look again at the passages you read in Lessons 1–5. What structures do you notice at work in those paragraphs?
- As you read (and write) during the next few days, be aware of the structure of each paragraph you come across. Try to identify the author's strategy; try to use different strategies in your own writing.

LANGUAGE AND STYLE

In most of the passages you have read so far, the author's ideas and intentions have been very clear. But what happens when they're not? What if the writer doesn't provide a topic sentence that clearly expresses the main idea? Or what if the writer gives you a poem instead of a clear-cut memorandum? How do you figure out what the author is trying to say?

The good news is that no matter how cryptic a piece of writing may seem, the author always leaves clues to help you figure out what he or she means. These clues can be found in the writer's **language** and **style**—the words the writer uses and the type of sentences in which he or she uses them. The next four lessons, therefore, focus on four different aspects of language and style:

- Point of view
- Diction
- Style
- Tone

You'll learn how authors use these elements to create meaning for their readers. Then you'll put it all together in Lesson 15 to see how language, style, structure, and meaning work together.

L · E · S · S · O · N

A MATTER OF PERSPECTIVE: POINT OF VIEW

11

LESSON SUMMARY

This lesson introduces you to the concept of *point of view,* one strategy writers use to convey their meaning to readers. Aspects such as whether writers use the more subjective *I* or the more objective *one,* whether they address readers as *you* or merely refer to an anonymous *they,* influence how readers understand what the writer has written.

icture this: You are walking along a tree-lined street late in the afternoon. Just ahead of you a woman is sitting on a bench; a dog lies in the shade at her feet. You watch them and nod hello as you walk by.

Now, picture this: You are that dog. You're sitting in the shade under a bench next to your owner's feet. Suddenly someone walks down the street in front of you. If you look up, you can see that person nod as he or she walks by.

Although you've just pictured the same thing—a person walking by a woman with a dog—you've really pictured two very different scenes, haven't you? The scenario looks quite different from the dog's point of view than from the walker's.

This shift in perspective happens in writing by changing the point of view. Point of view is one of the first choices writers make when they begin to write, because it is the point of view that determines who is speaking to the reader.

Point of view is the person or perspective through which the writer channels his or her information and ideas. Just as we may look at a physical object from a number of different perspectives (from above it, below it, behind it, beside it, and so on), we can look at information and ideas from different perspectives as well (mine, yours, his or hers, the professor's, the country's, and so on).

THREE KINDS OF POINT OF VIEW

When it comes to expressing point of view, writers can use three distinct approaches:

- **First person point of view** is a highly individualized, personal point of view in which the writer or narrator speaks about his or her own feelings and experiences directly to the reader using these pronouns: *I, me, mine; we, our, us.*
- **Second person point of view** is another personal point of view in which the writer speaks directly to the reader, addressing the reader as *you.*
- **Third person point of view** is an impersonal, objective point of view in which the perspective is that of an outsider (a "third person") who is not directly involved in the action. There is no direct reference to either the reader (second person) or the writer (first person). The writer chooses from these pronouns: *he, him, his; she, her, hers; it, its;* and *they, them, theirs.*

All of these points of view are available to writers, but not all of them may be appropriate for what they're writing, and only one of them will create the exact effect a writer desires. That's because each approach establishes a particular relationship between the reader and the writer.

WHEN WRITERS USE FIRST PERSON

Imagine you get one of the following messages from your company's head office:

A. The company congratulates you on the birth of your child.

B. We congratulate you on the birth of your child.

Which message would you rather receive?

Most of us would probably prefer to receive message B over message A. Why? What is the difference between these two messages? Both messages use the second person point of view, right? They both address the reader as "you." But you probably noticed that the writers chose different points of view to refer to themselves. Message A uses the third person point of view ("the company") whereas message B uses the first person pronoun "we." As a result, message B seems more sincere because it comes *from* a person *to* a person rather than from "the company" (a thing) to a person (*you*).

But the messages above do more than just express congratulations to the reader. They also seem to indicate something about how the people in the head office want to be perceived. In fact, their choice of point of view shows whether they want to be seen as people ("we") or as an entity ("the company"). Read the messages again and then decide how you think each writer wants to be perceived.

Which message seems to tell the reader, "We can speak directly to you because we are real people behind this company"?

Message _____

Which message seems to tell the reader, "We have a very formal relationship; let's not get too personal"?

Message _____

The company that sends message A suggests to the reader that "We have a very formal relationship; let's not get too close or too personal." Message B, on the other hand, tells the reader something more like this: "*We* can speak directly to *you* because we are real people behind this company." Thus, the point of view reflects the way the senders of the message wish to be perceived—as a distant entity (message A) or as friendly colleagues (message B).

DISTANCE VS. INTIMACY

Whether writers intend it or not (though they almost always do), the third person point of view establishes a certain distance between the writer and the reader. There's no direct person-to-person contact that way (*me* to *you*). Rather, with the third person point of view, someone (or something) else is speaking to the reader.

The first person point of view, on the other hand, establishes a certain intimacy between the writer and the reader. The writer uses *I, my, mine, we, our,* or *us* as if expressing his or her own personal feelings and ideas directly to the reader. "*We* congratulate you" makes message B much more personal than message A, where *the company* congratulates you.

- First person point of view establishes intimacy. The writer wants to be close to the reader.
- Third person point of view establishes distance. The writer wants to distance him- or herself from the reader.

WHEN WRITERS USE THIRD PERSON

In a business environment, it's not always practical to be personal. Though the first person point of view may make the reader feel close to the writer, the first person

point of view also implies a certain *subjectivity*. That is, the writer is expressing a very personal view from a very personal perspective.

SUBJECTIVITY VS. OBJECTIVITY

There's nothing wrong with expressing personal views, but in the business world, writers may not always be at an advantage using the first-person point of view. They're more likely to be taken seriously when they're *objective*, presenting things from an outsider's point of view, than when they're *subjective*, presenting things from their own possibly selfish or biased point of view.

- **Subjective**: based on the thoughts, feelings, and experiences of the speaker or writer (first person point of view)
- **Objective**: unaffected by the thoughts, feelings, and experiences of the speaker or writer (third person point of view)

Thus, if you wanted to complain about a new office policy, which of the following points of view do you think would be more effective?

A. I think our new office policy is a failure.
B. The new office policy appears to be a failure.

Most people would agree that sentence B is more effective. The question is, *why*?

1. The point of view of sentence B is more effective than that of sentence A because
   a. sentence A is too subjective
   b. sentence B is too subjective
   c. sentence A is too objective
   d. all of the above

The answer is **a**. Sentence A uses the first person point of view, and because *I* is so subjective and personal, it doesn't carry as much weight as the objective sentence

B. In sentence B, there is no personal perspective; someone from the outside (a third person, not the reader or the writer) is looking at the policy and evaluating it. The third person point of view is almost always considered to be more objective because the third person is not directly involved in the action. *I*, however, *is* directly involved in the action (the policy) and therefore cannot have an objective opinion about the policy's success or failure. *I*'s opinion may be prejudiced by the writer's personal experience.

Of course, even when a writer uses third person, he or she can still express his or her own opinion. When that opinion is expressed in the third person, however, it *appears* much more objective.

WHEN WRITERS USE SECOND PERSON

When is *you* an appropriate pronoun? What effect does it create for you, the reader? *You* generally is used to address the reader directly, particularly when the writer is giving directions. Imagine, for example, that you have just started a new job. On your first day of work, you receive the following memo:

Memo A

As a new employee, you need to take care of several items in your first week of work. First, you need to visit our Human Resources Office to complete your new employee file. Second, you need to visit our Payroll Office to be added to our payroll. Finally, you need to meet with your immediate supervisor to develop your first six-month statement of goals.

Now, imagine you receive this memo instead:

Memo B

New employees must take care of several items during their first week of work. First, they must go to the Human Resources Office to complete a new

employee file. Second, they must go to the Payroll Office to be added to the payroll. Finally, they must meet with their immediate supervisor to develop their first six-month statement of goals.

Which memo would you rather receive? _____

Most likely you'd rather receive Memo A. Now, here's the tougher question:

2. The point of view of Memo A is more effective than the point of view of Memo B because
   a. Memo A feels less formal
   b. Memo A speaks personally to the reader
   c. Memo A addresses the reader as an individual
   d. all of the above

Most people would prefer Memo A for all of these reasons, so the answer is **d.** First of all, in Memo A, the writer speaks directly to the reader (*you*). In Memo B, the writer speaks in the third person ("new employees"); the memo never acknowledges that *you* are a new employee. As a result, Memo B sounds more formal or official. The second person point of view, however, addresses you personally. It also singles you out as an individual, not as a category (new employees). It is almost like Memo A was written just for you.

SECOND PERSON AND AUDIENCE

In fact, because Memo A uses the second person point of view, you can make certain assumptions about the audience for this memo. Re-read Memo A and then answer this question:

3. Memo A was most likely written for
   a. all employees
   b. managers of new employees
   c. new employees only
   d. Human Resources employees

Because Memo A uses the second person pronoun *you*, you can assume that it is being given **c,** *only* to new employees. It must be, because it can't work for any other audience because of its pronoun.

Memo B, on the other hand, could be used for a much larger audience. In fact, the memo could be part of a larger document addressed to all employees, or it could be directed to all the people mentioned in the paragraph (new employees, Human Resources, Payroll personnel, and supervisors). So the third person point of view may have been used in Memo B not to create a distance between the reader and the writer, but to allow for a wider audience.

Writers may also use *you* to make readers feel as if they are taking part in the action or ideas being expressed in the text. For example, let's imagine that a writer wants to convince readers that a four-day work week is a good idea. The writer could use the third person point of view as in the following paragraph:

Paragraph A

Imagine how wonderful it would be if employees had a four-day work week. Rather than working five eight-hour days (40 hours), employees would work four ten-hour days (still 40 hours). Then, they would have Friday, Saturday, and Sunday off. This would give employees a three-day weekend *every week*. The benefits of this extra day would be numerous. Employees would have a full day for running errands that can't be done while they're at work; a day to clean while their kids are at school so that they could have leisurely family weekends; one less day of child care expenses they would have to pay; an extra day of rest. Psychologically, employees would also benefit by feeling that there's almost a fair balance in their lives between work (four days) and rest (three days).

Or the writer could use the second person point of view to express the same ideas.

Paragraph B

Imagine how wonderful it would be if you had a four-day work week. Rather than working five eight-hour days (40 hours), you'd work four ten-hour days (still 40 hours). Then, you'd have Friday, Saturday, and Sunday off. This would give you a three-day weekend *every week*. The benefits of this extra day would be numerous. You'd have a full day for running errands that you can't get done while you're at work; a day to clean while your kids are at school so that you could have leisurely family weekends; one less day of child care expenses you'd have to pay; an extra day for you to rest. Psychologically, you would also benefit by feeling that there's almost a fair balance in your life between work (four days) and rest (three days).

Did you notice the difference between the paragraphs? What pronouns does each paragraph use?

4. Paragraph A uses
    a. first person pronouns (*I, we*)
    b. second person pronouns (*you*)
    c. third person pronouns (*he, she, they*)

5. Paragraph B uses
    a. first person pronouns (*I, we*)
    b. second person pronouns (*you*)
    c. third person pronouns (*he, she, they*)

Paragraph A uses the third person (**c**), while Paragraph B uses second person (**b**). Now, which paragraph do you find more convincing? Most people would be more convinced by paragraph B. Why?

6. Paragraph B seems more convincing because
   a. "you" puts the readers into the action of the paragraph
   b. "you" makes readers pay more attention
   c. "you" makes readers imagine themselves in that situation
   d. all of the above

The second person point of view does all of these things (**d**), and that's why it is often more convincing than the other points of view. The second person point of view puts you, as a reader, directly into the situation. As soon as you read that word *you*, you start to pay extra attention because the writer is addressing you directly. And you can't help but imagine yourself enjoying the benefits of a four-day work week because the writer puts you in each scenario. The writer of this paragraph knows that if you imagine yourself in these situations, you are much more likely to see the benefits of a four-day work week.

SUMMARY

You can see by now how important point of view is in writing, for each point of view creates a certain effect. Sometimes it brings the reader and the writer closer together; sometimes it pushes them apart. Sometimes it makes an argument more convincing through third person objectivity; sometimes an argument is more convincing through second person involvement; and sometimes it's more convincing through first person intimacy. Writers choose their point of view carefully in order to create a certain relationship both with their ideas and with the reader.

Skill Building Until Next Time

- Imagine you have an argument with someone. Tell the story of the argument, first from your point of view using the first person pronoun. Then, tell the story from the other person's point of view, again using the first person pronoun. Finally, tell the story from an outsider's point of view using the third person pronoun. Notice how the story changes when the point of view changes, and notice how both first person accounts will be subjective while the third person account is objective.

- Take a memo or letter you received at work. If the information addresses you in the second person *you*, change it to a third person point of view (*employees, managers, clients*). Or, if the writer uses the first person point of view (*I* or *we*), change that to the third person point of view to eliminate the subjectivity.

L · E · S · S · O · N

DICTION: WHAT'S IN A WORD?

12

LESSON SUMMARY

Today's lesson focuses on *diction*, the words writers choose to convey their meaning. The smallest change in choice of words can significantly change the tone and meaning of a passage. Today's lesson shows you how to pick up on the clues to meaning writers give through their choice of words.

hat made Sherlock Holmes such a good detective? Was he just much smarter than everyone else? Did he have some sort of magical powers? Could he somehow see into the future or into the past? No, Sherlock Holmes was no medium or magician. So what was his secret?

His powers of observation.

You may recall that the introduction to this book talked about *active reading*. As an active reader, you should have been marking up the passages you've read in this book: identifying unfamiliar vocabulary, underlining key words and ideas, and recording your reactions and questions in the margin. But there's another part of active reading we haven't talked about: **making observations**.

MAKING OBSERVATIONS

Making observations means looking carefully at the text and noticing specific things about *how it is written*. You might notice, for example, the point of view the author has chosen. You could also notice:

- Particular words and phrases the writer uses
- The way those words and phrases are arranged in sentences and paragraphs
- Word or sentence patterns that are repeated
- Important details about people, places, and things

When you make observations, you can then make valid *inferences*. As a matter of fact, you did this in Lesson 11 when you made assumptions about how the writer wanted to be perceived based on the point of view he or she used.

OBSERVATIONS AND INFERENCES

Inferences, as you may recall, are conclusions based on reason, fact, or evidence. Good inferences come from good observations. The observations are the evidence for the inferences. Good inferences—ones based on careful observation—can help you determine meaning, as they helped Sherlock Holmes solve crimes.

To be better readers, then, we need to be more like Sherlock Holmes: We need to be better observers. In the story "The Adventure of the Blanched Soldier," Sherlock Holmes tells a client: "*I see no more than you, but I have trained myself to notice what I see.*" You don't have to be an Einstein to be a good reader; you just have to train yourself to notice what you see.

OBSERVING DICTION

Test your observation skills on the two sentences below:

A. The company's new attendance policy, which goes into effect on Monday, should significantly reduce absenteeism.

B. The company's draconian new attendance policy, which goes into effect on Monday, should significantly reduce absenteeism.

You don't need Sherlock Holmes's magnifying glass to see the difference between sentence A and sentence B: B uses the words *draconian* and *new* to describe the attendance policy, while A uses only *new*. (Go back to Lesson 3 if you've forgotten what *draconian* means.) Now that you have noticed this, why is it important?

1. What does sentence B tell you that sentence A doesn't?
   a. what type of policy is being discussed
   b. how the writer feels about the policy
   c. when the policy begins

The answer is **b**. Both sentences tell you that the policy is a new attendance policy, and both say that the policy goes into effect on Monday. But sentence B, because it adds the word *draconian,* tells you how the writer *feels* about the new policy: He doesn't like it. His opinion is implied through his choice of the word *draconian*. Rather than directly saying, "I think this policy is very severe," the writer *suggests* or *implies* that this is the way he feels.

DENOTATION AND CONNOTATION

Now, suppose sentence A also had another adjective to describe the new policy.

A. The company's firm new attendance policy, which goes into effect on Monday, should significantly reduce absenteeism.
B. The company's draconian new attendance policy, which goes into effect on Monday, should significantly reduce absenteeism.

Do the two sentences now mean the same thing? Yes and no. Both *firm* and *draconian* suggest that the policy is strict, but each word has a specific implication or suggested meaning about *how* strict that policy is. A *firm* policy is not as strict as a *draconian* policy. Furthermore, *draconian* suggests that the policy is not only strict but unfairly or unreasonably so.

So the words writers choose, even though they may mean the same thing when you look them up in the dictionary, actually have another level of meaning. This is called their **connotation**. *Connotation* is the implied meaning, the meaning that evolves when the dictionary definition (**denotation**) develops an emotional or social register or a suggestion of degree. The specific words writers choose—their *diction* or word choice—can therefore reveal a great deal about how authors feel about their subjects.

> **Diction: the particular words chosen and used by the author.**
> **Denotation: exact or dictionary meaning.**
> **Connotation: implied or suggested meaning.**

HOW DICTION INFLUENCES MEANING

Put your powers of observation to work on the following sentences. Read them carefully and then write down what you notice about each writer's specific choice of words. See if you can use the writers' diction to determine what they are inferring about the seriousness of the situation they are describing.

A. The political parties are meeting with the hopes of clearing up their differences.
B. The political parties have entered into negotiations in an attempt to resolve their conflict.

Both sentences convey the same information: Two parties are meeting because they have a disagreement of some sort to address. But the differences in the diction of each sentence tell us that these two situations aren't exactly the same—or at least that the two writers have different perceptions about the situations. What differences did you notice between these two sentences? List them below (an example has been provided to get you started):

Your Observations:

Example: *I noticed that sentence A says the political parties are "meeting" whereas sentence B says they "have entered into negotiations."*

Now that you've listed your observations, answer this question: In which sentence do you think the situation is more serious, and *why* do you think so? (The *why* is especially important.)

The difference in word choice should tell you that sentence B describes the more serious situation. Here are some of the observations you might have made about the writers' diction that would have told you so.

- The political parties in sentence B are not just "meeting," they've "entered into negotiations." This phrase is often used to describe disagreements between warring parties. And "negotiations" are much more formal than "meetings," suggesting that there is a serious difference to be resolved in sentence B.
- Whereas in sentence A they are ironing things out, the parties in sentence B only "attempt to" resolve the problems. This important difference suggests that the problem between the parties in sentence A is not that serious—the problem is likely to be resolved. In sentence B, on the other hand, "in an attempt" suggests that the problem is quite serious and that it will be difficult to resolve; the outlook is doubtful rather than hopeful.
- In sentence A, the parties are seeking to "clear up their differences," whereas in sentence B, the parties want to "resolve their conflict." The phrase "clear up" suggests that there is merely some sort of confusion between the two. However, "resolve"

suggests that there is a matter that must be solved or settled. And, of course, "conflict" indicates a more serious problem than "differences."

READING BETWEEN THE LINES

Looking at diction can be especially helpful when the writer's main idea isn't quite clear. For example, in the following paragraph—an excerpt from a letter of recommendation—the author doesn't provide a topic sentence that expresses her main idea. Instead, you must use your powers of observation to answer the question about how the author feels about the employee she describes.

Paragraph A

Jane Doe usually completes her work on time and proofreads it carefully. She is a competent typist and is familiar with several word processing programs. She has some knowledge of legal terminology and procedures which has been helpful.

2. What message does the writer of Paragraph A convey about Jane Doe?
   a. Jane Doe is an exceptional employee. Hire her immediately!
   b. Jane Doe is an average employee. She doesn't do outstanding work, but she won't give you any trouble.
   c. Jane Doe is a lousy worker. Don't even think about hiring her.

To answer this question, you made an inference. Now, support your inference with specific observations about the language in this paragraph. Why do you think your answer is correct? (An example has been provided to get you started.)

Your Observations and Inferences:

Example: *I noticed that the writer says Jane Doe "usually" completes her work on time (observation), which suggests that Jane Doe is good but not perfect; she doesn't always get her work done on schedule (inference).*

The diction of the paragraph best supports answer **b:** The writer feels that "Jane Doe is an average employee. She doesn't do outstanding work, but she won't give you any trouble." You might have supported this inference with observations like these:

- The writer uses the word *usually* in the first sentence, which means that Jane Doe is good, but not great; she doesn't always meet deadlines.
- The writer describes Jane Doe as a "competent" typist. This tells us that Jane Doe types well enough for the position, but she is not exceptional. She could be better.
- The writer tells us that Jane Doe is "familiar with" several word processing programs. This means that she can get by on those programs, but she is no expert and may have some trouble creating complex documents.
- The writer tells us that Jane Doe has "some knowledge of legal terminology and procedures," which tells us that Jane Doe knows a little, but not a lot; again, she's better than someone who knows nothing, but she's no expert.

Now, take a look at a revised letter of recommendation. The diction (the word choice) has been changed so that the paragraph sends a different message. Read the paragraph carefully and determine how this writer feels about Jane Doe.

Paragraph B

Jane Doe always submits her work promptly and proofreads judiciously. She is an excellent typist and has mastered several word processing programs. She also has an extensive knowledge of legal terminology and procedures, which has been invaluable.

3. What message does the writer of Paragraph B convey about Jane Doe?
   a. Jane Doe is an exceptional employee. Hire her immediately!
   b. Jane Doe is an average employee. She doesn't do outstanding work, but she won't give you any trouble.
   c. Jane Doe is a lousy worker. Don't even think about hiring her.

This time you should have chosen answer **a.** The change in diction tells you that this writer thinks Jane Doe is a fantastic employee. To be sure the difference in word choice is clear, write the words the writer of Paragraph B used to replace the words in Paragraph A. The first replacement has been filled in to get you started.

Paragraph A	Paragraph B
usually	always
on time	
carefully	
competent	
is familiar with	
some knowledge	
a help	

SUMMARY

Just as Sherlock Holmes learned to notice what he saw when he arrived at the scene of a crime, you, too, can learn to notice what you see when you look carefully at a piece of writing. By noticing the specific words a writer has chosen to use, you can help ensure that you fully comprehend the writer's message.

Skill Building Until Next Time

- Think about how you choose the words you use when you speak to people. Do you use different types of words for different people? Do you think carefully about what you say and which words you will use? How much are you aware of your own diction?

- Notice how much the meaning of a sentence can change when a single word is altered. Form a simple sentence, like: "Experts say the economy is *unhealthy*." Now, replace "unhealthy" with synonyms that have slightly different connotations, like: *sick, feeble, ill, dying, under the weather, feverish, infected*. Each word will express a slightly different attitude about your subject to the reader. Insert each of these words into your sentence and see how much the meaning is altered. (This exercise will work well if you choose words like *rich, tired, happy*, or *sad* that have many synonyms with a wide range of connotations.)

13

STYLE: IT'S NOT WHAT THEY SAY BUT HOW THEY SAY IT

LESSON SUMMARY

How a writer puts words together to express meaning is as important as *what* the writer says. This lesson shows you how to analyze the style of a piece of writing in order to get a better understanding of what the writer means.

Style?" you ask. "What does style have to do with reading comprehension?"

Actually, style has a good deal to do with reading comprehension. Just as writers use different structures to organize their ideas and information, they also use different styles to express their ideas and information. Thus, the more aware you are of the elements of style, the more successfully you can determine a writer's purpose and understand his or her ideas.

Style is also important because it is often what attracts us to, or repels us from, certain writers or types of writing. Though an awareness of style might not make us change our taste, it can at least help us appreciate different writers and different styles.

> Style: a distinctive way of writing or speaking or doing something; the manner in which something is done.

WHAT IS STYLE?

Style, in writing, generally consists of three elements:

- Sentence structure
- Degree of detail and description
- Degree of formality

Diction is also an aspect of style, but because diction is so essential to meaning, it had its own lesson in this book.

SENTENCE STRUCTURE

Looking at sentence structure means looking at the type of sentences the writer has used. Are they short, simple sentences? Or are they long and complex, with a lot of clauses and phrases? Or does the writer use a mix? Does every sentence sound the same, or is there variety in the word order and structure? Is the complexity or simplicity of the sentences at the right level for the readers?

Read the following sentences and then answer the questions that describe their sentence structure.

A. The meeting began. Mr. Thomas described the policy. Then Mr. Underwood spoke in favor of it. Afterward, Ms. Villegas spoke against it.

B. After the meeting, when everyone had already left the room, Ms. Villegas stayed behind to speak with Mr. Thomas. She carefully explained her position on the new policy, hoping she'd get him to change his mind.

1. Which version uses simple sentences?
   a. Version A
   b. Version B

2. Which version uses the same sentence structure throughout?
   a. Version A
   b. Version B

3. Which version uses complex sentences?
   a. Version A
   b. Version B

4. Which version varies the sentence structures, using different kinds of sentences?
   a. Version A
   b. Version B

You probably noticed that Version A is the one that uses simple sentences with essentially the same sentence structure throughout. (You might also have noticed that these sentences sound rather dull because they are so simple and unvaried.) In Version B, the sentences are far more complex with more variation in their structure.

DEGREE OF DETAIL AND DESCRIPTION

When you look at degree of detail and description, ask two things:

1. How specific is the author? Does he write "dog" (general) or "Labrador retriever" (specific detail)? Does she write "some" (general) or "three and a half pounds" (specific detail)?

2. How much description does the author provide? Does he write "Mr. B is my manager" (nondescriptive) or "Mr. B, my manager, is a

tall man with piercing eyes and a mustache" (descriptive)? Or does he go even further: "Mr. B, my manager, is six foot ten with eyes that pierce like knives and a mustache like Hitler's" (very descriptive)?

Try your hand at deciding whether words are specific and descriptive or general and nondescriptive.

5. Which words or phrases below are more specific and descriptive? Underline them. Which words or phrases are more general and nondescriptive? Circle them.
a. car
b. red 1968 Ford
c. on the corner of 58th and Broadway
d. on the corner

As you could probably tell, answers **b** and **c** are the more specific and descriptive ones, while answers **a** and **d** are more general and nondescriptive.

DEGREE OF FORMALITY

The **degree of formality** of a piece of writing has to do with how formal or casual the writer's language is. For example, does the writer use slang as if speaking to a friend, or jargon (specific, technical language) as if speaking to colleagues? Does the writer address the reader by his or her first name (casual), or by his or her title (formal)?

Decide whether the following sentences are formal or informal.

6. Which sentences below are more informal? Underline them. Which are more formal? Circle them.
a. Let's get together after work on Thursday.

b. We kindly request that you join us for a social gathering at the close of business on Thursday.
c. These figures indicate the sales have increased significantly.
d. Sales are up!

Chances are that you didn't have much trouble deciding that sentences **a** and **d** are more informal and sentences **b** and **c** are more formal.

HOW THE THREE ELEMENTS OF STYLE WORK TOGETHER

Look at how these three elements of style work together in the following examples. Below are two different letters. Both convey essentially the same information, but they are written in radically different styles. Read the letters carefully and then list your observations. What do you notice that's different between these two letters?

Letter A
Bob:
Listen, a while ago we rush ordered some paper from you. We haven't gotten it yet. What happened? Where is it? Find out! We need it!
—Joe

Letter B
Dear Mr. Brown:
Three weeks ago, on January 22, we rush ordered two dozen boxes of XYZ bond paper from you (Order #123456). To date we have not received our order. Please look into this matter immediately as we are in dire need of this product.
Sincerely,
Mr. White

What did you notice about these two letters? How are they different? Consider sentence structure, degree of description and detail, and degree of formality. List your observations below (an example has been provided to get you started):

Your Observations:

Example: *I notice that Letter A addresses the reader as "Bob" whereas Letter B addresses him as "Mr. Brown."*

Now, answer the following questions.

7. Which letter is more formal?
a. Letter A
b. Letter B

8. Which letter seems to have been written by someone who knows the recipient well?
a. Letter A
b. Letter B

9. In which letter is the sentence structure more complex?
a. Letter A
b. Letter B

10. Which letter is more descriptive and detailed?
a. Letter A
b. Letter B

You probably noticed immediately the difference in degree of formality between these two letters. Letter A is written in a very casual style, as if the writer knows the reader very well and therefore does not need to use a professional approach. Our first clue to this casual relationship is the way the letter is addressed. Letter A addresses the reader as "Bob" while letter B begins with a formal "Dear Mr. Brown." The same difference can be seen in the closing of the letters: "Joe" vs. "Sincerely, Mr. White."

The (in)formality of each relationship is also reflected in the sentence structure and degree of description and detail. You probably noticed, for example, that Letter A uses short, choppy sentences, and exclamation points, which make the letter sound less formal, more urgent, and more demanding. The writer also uses casual words like "listen" so that the writing sounds conversational. On the other hand, Letter B uses longer, more complex sentences to make the letter sound more formal and sophisticated.

At the same time you probably noticed that letter A does not provide specific information as Letter B does. Letter A tells us the writer placed an order for "some paper" "a while ago," but Letter B tells us the order was placed "three weeks ago, on January 22" and that the order was for "two dozen boxes of XYZ bond paper." The fact that Letter A does not provide specific details is further evidence that the reader knows the writer very well, for the writer doesn't have to provide specific details. Furthermore, in Letter A the writer uses a command—"Find out!"—whereas in Letter B, the writer *asks*, rather than demands, that the matter be looked into. This politeness reflects a professional distance between writer and reader.

In business, as in most writing, the audience usually determines the writer's style. The writer of Letter A is probably capable of writing in the style of Letter B, but because he has a casual relationship with his reader, he doesn't need to use a formal style.

THE EFFECT OF DESCRIPTION AND DETAIL

In business, what some people call "flowery" style—lots of description and detail—is almost never appropriate. Why? Because in business, as they say, "time is money," so readers don't want to spend time reading lengthy descriptions or extensive detail. They just want the facts: when the meeting will be held and where; what the new product is designed to do and how much it costs; how the new training manual is coming along. In most cases, the more straightforward, the better.

Other times, however, when they want readers to imagine a situation or to experience something through language, writers need a "flowery" style. That is, they need a high degree of description and detail. The two paragraphs below show the difference. Both describe the same business meeting, but in two very different styles. One is written in a style appropriate to business and only records the facts. The other describes the meeting in a style appropriate for general readers interested in the feelings of the employee, Mr. Newman.

Paragraph A

Yesterday at 9:00 A.M., Mr. Owen called Mr. Newman into his office. Mr. Owen reviewed Mr. Newman's personnel file. He congratulated Mr. Newman on his perfect attendance record and consistently satisfactory reviews. Then Mr. Owen informed Mr. Newman that his position, along with several others, was being eliminated due to a restructuring of the company. Mr. Owen offered Mr. Newman three months severance pay and continuation of benefits for one year.

Paragraph B

At 9:00 A.M., Mr. Owen raised a thick arm to wave Mr. Newman into his office. Mr. Newman obeyed reluctantly and sat stiffly in front of the monstrous oak desk that managed to dwarf even Mr. Owen, a bulky man with a protruding stomach. Mr. Newman fidgeted as Mr. Owen opened his personnel file. Then, after praising Mr. Newman for his years of perfect attendance and his continuously satisfactory reviews, Mr. Owen told Mr. Newman that his position—which he had had for over fourteen years—was being eliminated. The company was being restructured and Mr. Newman's job was no longer necessary.

Mr. Owen went on to explain that Mr. Newman would have three months of severance pay and a year of continued benefits, but Mr. Newman didn't hear him. He walked out of Mr. Owen's office before Mr. Owen could finish his sentence.

Now, write down your observations about these two paragraphs below. How are these two versions different? What did you notice about the sentence structure? About the degree of description and detail? About the degree of formality?

Your Observations:

Example: *I noticed that Version B is almost twice as long as Version A.*

Now, use your observations to answer the following questions.

11. Which version tells you more about Mr. Owen?

    a. Paragraph A

    b. Paragraph B

12. Which version tells you more about Mr. Newman?

    a. Paragraph A

    b. Paragraph B

13. Which version is more objective?

    a. Paragraph A

    b. Paragraph B

14. Which version makes you feel badly for Mr. Newman?

    a. Paragraph A

    b. Paragraph B

You noticed, of course, that Paragraph B is much more descriptive than Paragraph A—it tells you more about both Mr. Owen and Mr. Newman. Paragraph A just provides the facts—specific details, but no description. Paragraph A is very objective. We do not know what Mr. Owen looks like or how Mr. Newman feels (though we might be able to guess).

Paragraph B, however, tells us about Mr. Owen's appearance (he's a "thick," "bulky" man with a "protruding stomach"); we know about his desk (it's "monstrous"). More importantly, we know how Mr. Newman felt about the meeting and the news he received. Obviously, Mr. Newman knew he was going to get bad news; he entered the office "reluctantly" and "fidgeted" in his chair. Of course, he was very upset by the news, which he demonstrated by walking out of the room before Mr. Owen could finish. These details help us feel something for Mr. Newman because the characters and the situation are presented visually; we can almost see what happens.

SUMMARY

Style, as you can see, is an important aspect of reading comprehension. It can tell us about the writer's relationship to the reader; it can distance us with its objectivity or draw us in with its description and detail. As readers, we tend to react strongly to style, often without knowing why. But now you do know why, and you can use that knowledge to help you understand what you read.

Skill Building Until Next Time

- As you come across sentences or paragraphs written in different styles, see how they would sound if the style were altered. Change the level of formality, the degree of description and detail, or the sentence structure to create a new style.

- Do you have a favorite author? Take a second look at a particularly memorable work by this author, paying close attention to the style elements at work. If you are a Jane Austen fan, pick out features that make her novels enjoyable for you. Do you like her degree of formality, the way she uses detail to describe fancy parties, or the way she varies her sentence structure? After you've taken a close look at this work, try your own hand at it. Can you write a letter to a friend in the same style that Jane Austen would have? How about Ernest Hemingway or Stephen King?

HOW THEY SAY IT, PART TWO: TONE

14

LESSON SUMMARY

The way you perceive a person's tone of voice has a great deal to do with how you understand what that person is saying. The same is true of tone in writing; it's vital to pick up on clues to tone in order to understand a written piece fully. This lesson shows you how.

ay this word out loud: "Sure."

How did you say it? Did you say it with a smile, as in "Sure, any time"? Or did you say it flatly, as if responding to a command? Or did you stretch the word out, "*Suuuurre,*" as if you didn't believe what someone just said? Or did you ask it, as in, "Are you *sure* this is okay?"

Perhaps you didn't realize there were so many ways to say this one single word, "sure." But there are. Why? The word itself isn't different; its denotation (dictionary meaning) isn't different; so how can the same word express so many different things?

The difference in the meaning of all of these *sure*s comes from the tone—how you say the word, and thus how your listeners will feel when they hear you say it.

Tone: the mood or attitude conveyed by words or speech.

When you speak and listen, you can hear the tone of your own and the other's voice. But how do you catch tone in writing? How do you know how the writer wants his or her words to sound? "Sure" by itself doesn't tell us whether you should whisper or shout it out. You need to look at the context surrounding that word to find clues about the proper tone to use.

Think about how tone is created in speech. When you say "sure," the tone changes according to how loudly or softly you say the word and how slowly or quickly you say it. Tone is also conveyed (or supported) by the speaker's expressions and body language. In writing, of course, you do not have these visual resources, but you do have plenty of clues to help you determine tone. Those clues come from the elements of language and style that you've studied so far: point of view, diction, and style.

HOW TONE INFLUENCES MEANING

It may help you to think of a sentence as a collection of ingredients (words and phrases) that result in a dish (idea). These elements of language and style are like the spices that you need to give that sentence a certain flavor. Different spices will result in a different flavor (tone).

Look at the two letters below. Both convey essentially the same information, but they have two rather different tones.

Letter A
Dear Client:

Thank you for your letter. We will take your suggestion into consideration. We appreciate your concern.

Letter B
Dear Valued Customer:

Thank you for your recent letter regarding our refund policy and procedure. We are taking your suggestion quite seriously and truly appreciate your concern.

Which of these letters has a more positive tone? As you can see, Letter B is more positive. Why? What do you notice about Letter B that is different from Letter A? List your observations below:

Your Observations:

Example: *I noticed that Letter A is addressed "Dear Client" while Letter B is addressed "Dear Valued Customer."*

Perhaps you noticed that Letter B uses key words like "*valued* customer" and "*truly* appreciate." Letter B also refers to the specific contents of the reader's letter, thus letting the reader know that his or her letter has been read. Furthermore, Letter B tells the reader not just that the company "will take your suggestion into consideration"—which sounds a bit like an empty promise—but that the writers are taking the suggestion "quite seriously."

You may also notice that the sentences in Letter B are longer than those in Letter A, whose sentences are shorter and somewhat choppy. If you read those short sentences out loud, how do they sound? They're not very inviting, are they? They sound somewhat mechanical and empty of any feeling.

Use your observations to answer the questions below.

1. The tone of Letter A is best classified as
   a. sincere
   b. complimentary
   c. indifferent

Choice c, indifferent, best describes the tone of Letter A. There is no indication that the writers of Letter A have actually read their client's letter, so there's no indication that they plan to take the client's suggestion seriously. They are indifferent to it. Also, the sentence structure indicates that the writers have not put much thought into writing this letter; as a result, the sentences sound abrupt and even unappreciative.

2. The tone of letter B is best classified as
   a. cheerful
   b. sincere
   c. apologetic

In contrast to Letter A, the writers of Letter B are **b,** sincere. They know exactly what their customer wrote about—there's the importance of specific details again! They've also taken the time to individualize the letter; and they've added words that show they value their customer and their customer's feedback.

VARIETIES OF TONE

Just as there are endless varieties of tone when we speak, there are endless varieties of tone in writing.

Here's a short list of some of the more common words used to describe a writer's tone:

cheerful	sarcastic
complimentary	ironic
hopeful	wistful
sad	foreboding
gloomy	playful
apologetic	sincere
critical	insincere
insecure	authoritative
disrespectful	threatening
humorous	indifferent

If any of these terms are unfamiliar to you, please look them up in a dictionary right away.

PRACTICE

Now look at several sentences and paragraphs to see if you can correctly identify their tone. As you read them, think of how the paragraphs sound. You may even want to read them out loud. With what kind of voice do you read? What's your tone? Use your instincts, as well as your observations, to choose the correct tone for each paragraph. Answers and explanations come immediately after the practice paragraphs.

3. I think the theme of this novel probably has something to do with revenge.
   a. playful
   b. uncertain
   c. cheerful

4. Without a doubt, the theme of this novel is revenge.
   a. gloomy
   b. disrespectful
   c. authoritative

5. Your essay? Oh, it was just fabulous. Really, I've never seen anything like it.
   a. insincere
   b. critical
   c. disrespectful

6. This is one of the best essays I've ever seen. It's clear, concise, and convincing.
   a. complimentary
   b. wistful
   c. hopeful

7. Bill had stayed up all night preparing for this presentation. He had everything ready: charts, graphs, lists, statistics. This was the biggest meeting of his career. He was ready. He smiled as the cab pulled up to 505 Park Avenue, and he gave the taxi driver an extra large tip. He entered the building confidently and pushed #11 on the elevator. Suddenly, as the doors of the elevator closed, he realized that he had left his briefcase in the cab.
   a. cheerful
   b. ironic
   c. critical

Answers and Explanations

3. b. The writer is obviously afraid to be authoritative and uses phrases like "I think," "probably," and "something to do with," to reflect this uncertainty.

4. c. The writer is clearly comfortable in making a definitive statement. There is no hesitation in the tone here. Instead of suggesting, the writer declares: "Without a doubt…."

5. a. Because of the opening question and because the next sentences are so vague, a reader can assume that the writer either hasn't read the essay or didn't like it. Also, "really" indicates that the writer is afraid the reader won't be convinced by the statement, so he tries to emphasize it. Furthermore, "I've never seen anything like it" isn't necessarily a compliment—it could really mean many different things, not all of them good.

6. a. Unlike question 5 above, this paragraph really is complimentary. The writer specifies three things that make the reader's essay exceptional: It's "clear, concise and convincing." The use of more specific adjectives makes this writer's praise seem sincere.

7. b. *Irony* is the mood created when things happen in a manner that is opposite of what was expected to happen. Here, Bill had prepared diligently for the big meeting and had everything ready. But contrary to his expectations of having a very successful presentation, he had no presentation at all because he left his materials in the taxi cab. The irony is heightened by his confidence.

SUMMARY

An ability to determine tone is an essential component of reading comprehension. Often, writers will let their tone convey their meaning, so you need to look carefully for clues in the writer's language and style to determine how writers want their words to sound.

Skill Building Until Next Time

- Listen carefully to people today and notice how much you depend on tone to determine exactly what people mean when they speak to you. Notice also how you use tone to convey meaning when you speak to other people.
- Go back to the practice exercise where you identified the tone of those five passages. Try changing the tone of some of those passages.

L·E·S·S·O·N

WORD POWER: PUTTING IT ALL TOGETHER

15

LESSON SUMMARY

This lesson pulls together what you've learned in Lessons 11–14, as well as in previous lessons. It shows you how to use point of view, diction, style, and tone to understand what a writer means.

ou've learned a lot this week about language and how much it affects meaning. Before you add this knowledge to the knowledge you already have about structure and the basics of reading comprehension, take a minute for a brief review of the last four lessons. It's always a good idea to stop and review material you've learned before you go on to new material.

REVIEW: LANGUAGE AND STYLE

Point of view is the perspective from which the writer speaks. Sometimes writers use the first person point of view (*I, me, my, we, our, us*) to express their personal feelings and experiences directly to the reader. This point of view creates a sense of intimacy between the reader and the writer because it expresses an extremely subjective perspective. When writers use the second person point of view, they address the reader directly by using the pronoun *you*. This point of view is often used to give directions and to make the reader feel directly involved in the action described by the writer. The third person point of view is the objective perspective of a "third person," someone who is not directly involved in the action or ideas expressed in the passage. This point of view establishes a distance between the reader and writer and uses the pronouns *he, his, him, she, hers, her, it, its, they, them,* and *their*.

Diction refers to the specific words chosen by the author to express his or her ideas. Because words have both a *denotation* (exact or dictionary meaning) and a *connotation* (implied or suggested meaning), as well as an emotional register, the words an author chooses are very significant. Authors, like politicians, must choose their words carefully to express exactly the right idea with exactly the right impact.

Style is the manner in which the writers express their ideas in writing. Style is composed of three main elements: sentence structure, degree of description and detail, and degree of formality. Some writers use a very formal style; others may write in a casual style. Certain styles are best for particular audiences or purposes. For example, a high degree of formality with specific details but without any unneccessary description would be appropriate for business, where time is money and writers should get to the point as quickly as possible.

Finally, **tone** is the mood or attitude conveyed by the writing. Tone is created by a combination of point of view, diction, and style. Tone is extremely important in determining meaning because as we noted, a word as simple as "sure" can have many different meanings depending upon the tone in which it is said. To determine the tone, you have to look for clues as to how the writer wants his or her words to sound.

If any of these terms or ideas sound unfamiliar to you, STOP. Please take a few minutes to review whatever lesson is unclear.

PRACTICE

In today's practice, you'll combine the above aspects of language with everything else you've learned in this book about reading comprehension:

- Finding the facts
- Determining the main idea
- Determining vocabulary meaning through context
- Distinguishing facts and opinions
- Chronological order
- Cause and effect
- Compare and contrast
- Order of importance

PRACTICE PASSAGE 1

Begin with a paragraph someone might see in a company newsletter: a profile of a company executive. Read the paragraph carefully, marking it up as you go, and write your observations in the space provided.

Ms. A has been a dedicated employee since the company opened its doors in 1978. She started out as a clerk and quickly moved up in the ranks to become a branch manager in 1987. Her innovative revision of the marketing plan in 1988 doubled company profits within a year and earned her the position of Junior Vice President. Today she is a Senior Vice President who continues to contribute cutting-edge ideas and dedication to the company.

Your Observations:

Now answer the following questions.

1. Ms. A became a branch manager in
   a. 1987
   b. 1988
   c. 1978

2. Which sentence best sums up the main idea of this paragraph?
   a. Ms. A is a very smart.
   b. Ms. A is very dedicated.
   c. The company would be nowhere without Ms. A.

3. "Ms. A has been a dedicated employee since the company opened its doors in 1978" is
   a. fact
   b. opinion
   c. point of view

4. "Innovative" means
   a. helpful
   b. remarkable
   c. inventive

5. This paragraph is organized according to what structure?
   a. cause and effect
   b. compare and contrast
   c. chronological order
   d. order of importance

6. This paragraph uses what point of view?
   a. First person point of view
   b. Second person point of view
   c. Third person point of view

Answers

1. a. "She started out as a clerk and quickly moved up in the ranks to become a branch manager in 1987."

2. b. While it does seem that Ms. A must be very smart since she has had such success with the company, that is not the idea that governs the whole paragraph. Instead, the paragraph highlights her dedication by showing that she has been with the company since its beginning. Answer c can't be correct because, although the paragraph indicates that Ms. A is very valuable, it does not say that the company would be nowhere without her. This is an inference you might make but cannot support.

3. b. Although the sentence does contain fact (she started with the company in 1978), the sentence makes an assertion about those years since 1978: that Ms. A has been dedicated all those years. This is an assertion, an opinion that needs evidence. The rest of the paragraph goes on to provide that evidence.

4. c. The best clue to determining the meaning of this word is found in the last sentence, which says that Ms. A "continues to contribute cutting-edge ideas" to the company. Since the paragraph only mentions one specific contribution (the one labeled "innovative"), we can assume that *innovative* means *cutting-edge* or *inventive*.

5. c. The paragraph follows Ms. A's career with the company from its start in 1978 to the present.

6. c. This paragraph uses the objective third person point of view. There is no *I* or *we* (first person) or *you* (second person), and the only pronouns the paragraph uses are the third person pronouns *she* and *her*.

How did you do? If you got all six answers correct, good work. The table below shows you which lesson to study for each question you missed.

If you missed:	Then study:
Question 1	Lesson 1
Question 2	Lesson 2
Question 3	Lesson 4
Question 4	Lesson 3
Question 5	Lesson 6
Question 6	Lesson 11

PRACTICE PASSAGE 2

Now try another paragraph. Don't forget to mark it up as you read and make observations. Pay special attention to language and style.

There will be dire consequences for employees if the company goes through with the merger. First of all, the merger will mean that many of us will have to relocate if we want to keep our jobs. Second, many of us will be transferred to new departments to fill the needs of the new conglomerate. But most importantly, a merger means that hundreds of us will lose our jobs as the companies collapse, such as payroll and the human resources departments.

7. The main idea of this passage is that the budget cuts would
   a. be great for the university
   b. not change things much
   c. be bad for employees

8. A "conglomerate" is
   a. a corporation made up of several different companies
   b. a large department
   c. the person in charge of a merger or acquisition

9. This passage is organized
   a. in chronological order
   b. by cause and effect
   c. by order of importance
   d. both a and c
   e. both b and c

10. This passage uses which point of view?
   a. first person
   b. second person
   c. third person

page note unreadable

11. This passage is written from whose perspective?
a. that of the employers
b. that of the employees
c. that of an outside consultant

12. The choice of the word *dire* suggests that the consequences of the merger would be
a. minimal
b. expected
c. disastrous

13. Which word best describes the style of this passage?
a. informal, conversational
b. descriptive, story-like
c. formal, business-like

14. The tone of this passage is
a. sad
b. foreboding
c. threatening

Answers

7. c. The first sentence is the topic sentence, which establishes that the merger will be bad for employees. The remaining sentences support that idea.

8. a. This paragraph tells us that the company will be a "conglomerate" after the merger, when two or more companies will be joined into one. Therefore, the company will be one large corporation made up of other smaller corporations.

9. e. The writer warns readers of the effects a merger would have on employees and arranges those effects in order of importance, saving the most important effect for last.

10. a. The first person point of view is reflected in the use of the pronoun *us* and *we*.

11. b. The writer says that the merger will have "dire consequences" for the employees and then uses the pronouns *us* and *we*—identifying himself with the employees—when listing those dire consequences.

12. c. The effects the writer includes here are all very serious, especially the third effect—unemployment. The writer has chosen the word *dire* to emphasize that seriousness.

13. c. The passage avoids any unnecessary description or details and uses formal rather than casual language.

14. b. Each sentence explains a negative effect that the merger will have on the employees and the negativity of this passage is heightened by the words "dire" and "collapse." Though the merger itself might be described as *threatening* (choice c), the writer is not threatening anybody.

How did you do? Once again, congratulations if you got them all correct. If not, the table below tells you what to do.

If you missed:	Then study:
Question 7	Lesson 2
Question 8	Lesson 3
Question 9	Lessons 7 and 9
Question 10	Lesson 11
Question 11	Lesson 11
Question 12	Lesson 12
Question 13	Lesson 13
Question 14	Lesson 14

Skill Building Until Next Time

- Review the Skill Building sections from Lessons 6–14. Try any Skill Builders you didn't do.
- Write a paragraph about what you've learned in the last two weeks about structure and language. Begin your paragraph with a clear topic sentence, such as "I've learned a lot about how writers use structure and language." Then, write several sentences that support or explain your assertion. Try to use at least one new vocabulary word in your paragraph.

READING BETWEEN
THE LINES

ow that you've studied the way authors use structure and language to organize and express their ideas, you're ready to tackle more difficult passages: those in which the writers don't provide clear topic sentences or do not clearly indicate their intentions. To understand this type of text, you have to "read between the lines." This means you have to really put your observation skills to use and scour the passage for clues to meaning. Like Sherlock Holmes, you will really have to notice what you see.

By the end of this section, you should be able to:

- Determine an implied main idea
- Determine an implied cause or effect
- Distinguish between logical and emotional appeals
- Determine the theme of a piece of literature

You'll look at a variety of texts, including some literature, and then put it all together in a review lesson.

L·E·S·S·O·N
FINDING THE IMPLIED MAIN IDEA
16

LESSON SUMMARY

This lesson shows you how to determine the main idea of a passage in which the writer has not provided a topic sentence or otherwise spelled it out for you.

O
h, the power of suggestion. Advertisers know it well—and so do writers. They know that they can get an idea across to their readers without directly saying it. Instead of providing a topic sentence that expresses their main idea, many times they simply omit that sentence and instead provide a series of clues through structure and language to get their ideas across.

Finding an implied main idea is much like finding a stated main idea. If you recall from Lesson 2, a main idea is defined as an assertion about the subject that controls or holds together all of the ideas in the passage. Therefore, the main idea must be general enough to encompass all of the ideas in the passage. Much like a net, it holds everything in the passage together. So far, all but one of the passages in this book have had a topic sentence that stated the main idea, so finding the main idea was something of a process of elimination: You could eliminate the sentences that weren't general enough to encompass the whole passage. But what do you do when there's no topic sentence?

You use your observations to make an inference—this time, an inference about the main idea or point of the passage.

HOW TO FIND AN IMPLIED MAIN IDEA

Finding an implied main idea requires you to use your observations to make an inference that, like a topic sentence, encompasses the whole passage. It might take a little detective work, but now that you know how to find details and how to understand word choice, style, and tone, you can make observations that will enable you to find main ideas even when they're not explicitly stated.

PRACTICE PASSAGE 1

For the first example of finding an implied main idea, let's return to our friend Mr. Blank. If you remember, back in Lesson 1 his apartment was robbed. Now look at a statement from the building manager in response to news of the robbery:

> This is the third robbery in our building this month. Each time, the thieves have gotten past building security with almost the entire contents of the victim's apartment. Yet each time, the security officers say they have seen nothing unusual.

> Now, there is no topic sentence in this paragraph, but you should be able to determine the manager's main idea from the facts he provides and from his tone. What is he suggesting?

1. Which of the following best summarizes the manager's main idea?
   a. There are too many robberies in the building.
   b. There are not enough security officers in the building.
   c. There is something wrong with the security in the building.

Answer

The correct answer is **c**, "There is something wrong with the security in the building." How can you tell that this is the main idea? For one thing, it's the only one of the three choices that is general enough to serve as a "net" for the paragraph; choice **a** is implied only in the first sentence and choice **b** isn't mentioned at all. In addition, each sentence on its own suggests that security in the building has not been working properly. Furthermore, the word "yet" indicates that there is a conflict between the events that have taken place and the duties of the security officers.

PRACTICE PASSAGE 2

Now examine the following statement from Mr. Blank's neighbor, who was also interviewed after the robbery:

> Well, Mr. Blank's a pretty carefree man. A few times I've knocked on his door and he just hollers, "Come in," and I just have to push the door open because it isn't locked. He often forgets things, too, like where he parked his car or where he put his keys. One time I found him in the hall searching through his bags because he couldn't find his keys, and it turned out the door was open anyway. Sometimes I wonder how he remembers to eat, let alone to take care of his apartment.

2. What is Mr. Blank's neighbor suggesting?
   a. Mr. Blank forgets everything.
   b. Mr. Blank may have left his door open that day.
   c. Mr. Blank is too carefree for his own good.

You can attack the question this way: Which of these three statements do the sentences in the neighbor's statement support? Try a process of elimination. Do all of the sentences support choice **a**? If not, cross **a** out. Do all of the sentences support choice **b**? Choice **c**?

Answer

The correct answer is **b,** "Mr. Blank may have left his door open that day." How can you tell? Because this is the only idea that all of the sentences in the neighbor's statement support. You know that Mr. Blank often doesn't lock his door when he's home; you also know that he often forgets things. Thus, the neighbor's statement contains both **a** and **c,** but neither can be the main idea because the neighbor discusses both things in combination. This combination makes it likely that Mr. Blank left his apartment door open on the day he was robbed.

PRACTICE PASSAGE 3

Now look at a paragraph in which the *language* the writer uses is what enables you to determine meaning. Back in Lesson 13, you read a thumbnail sketch of Mr. B the manager. Below is a more detailed version of that description. Read the following paragraph carefully and see if you can determine the implied main idea of the paragraph.

> Mr. B, my manager, is six feet ten inches tall with eyes that pierce like knives and a mustache like Hitler's. He invades the office at precisely 8:00 every morning demanding this report and that report. He spends half of the day looking over my shoulder and barking orders. And whenever there's a mistake—even if it's his fault—he blames it on me.

Before you decide on the implied main idea, list your observations. What did you notice about the language in this paragraph? An example is provided to get you started.

Your Observations:

Example: *I noticed that Mr. B's eyes are compared to knives.*

3. Which of the following best expresses the implied message of the passage?
   a. Working for Mr. B is a challenge.
   b. Working for Mr. B is like working for a tyrant.
   c. Mr. B is a terrible manager.

Answer

The correct answer is **b,** "Working for Mr. B is like working for a tyrant." There are many clues in the language of this paragraph that lead you to this inference. First, you probably noticed that Mr. B "has eyes that pierce like knives." This comparison (called a *simile*) suggests that Mr. B does not look at others very warmly; instead, his eyes stab.

Second, the description of Mr. B's mustache is a critical part of the way the author establishes the tone of this paragraph. To say that Mr. B has a mustache "like Hitler's" automatically makes us picture Mr. B as Hitler. This is a very serious comparison (also a simile). A writer wouldn't compare someone to Hitler—even on a physical level—unless he wanted to paint that person as evil.

Third, the author tells us that Mr. B "invades" the office at "precisely" 8:00 every morning. "Invade" is a key word choice. The author could have said that Mr. B "storms into" the office or "barges into" the office, but he chose the word "invades," as if Mr. B doesn't belong there or as if Mr. B is attempting to take over territory that isn't his. Furthermore, Mr. B spends the day "barking orders," and, like a tyrant, he passes the blame onto others when something goes wrong. Thus, though answers **a** and **c** may be true—it must be a challenge to work with Mr. B, and he doesn't seem to be the best "people person"—answer **b** is the only idea that all of the sentences in the paragraph support.

Of course, this person's description of Mr. B is very subjective, using as it does the first person point of view. As an active reader, you should wonder whether everyone sees Mr. B this way or if this employee is unable to be objective about Mr. B.

PRACTICE PASSAGE 4

Many people find reading literature a difficult task because in literature (fiction, drama, and poetry), the main idea is almost never expressed in a clear topic sentence. Instead, readers have to look for clues that are often hidden in the language of the text. For example, the following fictional paragraph describes a character. Read it carefully, make your observations, and then identify the main idea of the paragraph.

In the evening when Dell finished a long day at work, she came home alone to an empty house. She'd make herself a small tasteless supper—she never felt like cooking anymore, now that there was no one else but her to feed. At night she'd tend to the animals in the back and would often talk to them to break the silence that imprisoned her.

Your Observations:

Example: *I noticed that Dell is the only person mentioned in this paragraph.*

4. The main idea of this paragraph is that
   a. Dell wants to be alone
   b. Dell was abandoned
   c. Dell is very lonely

Answer

Although it is possible that **b**, "Dell was abandoned," there is no evidence in this paragraph to support that inference. Thus, **b** cannot be the main idea. Answer **a**, "Dell wants to be alone," cannot be correct either, since everything in the paragraph suggests that Dell does *not* like to be alone: She doesn't like to cook anymore now that she's alone, and she talks to the animals because there's no one else for her to talk to.

Furthermore, the language of the paragraph creates a feeling of intense loneliness: Dell comes home "alone" to an "empty" house; her dinner is "tasteless"; she talks to the animals "to break the silence that imprison[s] her." All of these words work together in the paragraph to create a feeling of loneliness. Thus, without directly saying so, the writer tells us that **c**, "Dell is very lonely."

SUMMARY

Many writers use implication to convey meaning rather than directly stating their ideas. This is especially true in literature, where readers generally prefer suggestion to direct statements. Finding the implied main idea requires a little detective work, but it is not as difficult as you may have thought, now that you know more about language and the way words can be used to suggest ideas.

Skill Building Until Next Time

- Listen carefully to people today. Are there times when they *imply* things without directly saying them? Are there times when *you* use suggestion to get your ideas across? How do you do this? Be aware of how you and others use indirect language and suggestion to convey meaning.

- Write a paragraph that does not have a topic sentence. You should have a clear idea of the main idea before you write your paragraph and make sure your sentences use language that will help your readers understand your main idea. For example, think of a topic sentence about the kind of person you are, but don't write it down. Then, write several sentences that support your topic sentence with language that leads your reader to the proper conclusion. You may want to show your paragraph to others to see if they can correctly infer your main idea.

L · E · S · S · O · N

ASSUMING CAUSES AND PREDICTING EFFECTS

17

LESSON SUMMARY

Today's lesson focuses on how to determine cause and effect when they are only implied, rather than explicitly stated.

ave you ever regretted just "telling it like it is"? Many times you can't come right out and say what you'd like, but, like writers, you can get your ideas across through *implication* or inference.

This lesson focuses on two specific types of implication: reading between the lines to *determine cause* and reading between the lines to *predict effects*.

In case you need a reminder: A *cause* is the person or thing that makes something happen or produces an effect. An *effect* is the change that occurs as a result of some action or cause. Cause tells us why something happened; effect tells us what happened after a cause (or series of causes).

DETERMINING IMPLIED CAUSES

In order to see how to determine causes that are implied rather than stated, look at the following brief fictional passage. Read the passage carefully and actively. After you make your observations, see if you can use the writer's clues to determine why the characters are fighting.

Anne sat with her feet up on the couch, drinking a Coke. She heard footsteps by the front door. Brenda was right on time, as usual. Never a minute early or late—for her, everything was very exact.

Anne placed her feet on the floor, reached for the remote and turned off the television. She knew Brenda would demand her complete attention. She knew Brenda would hang up her coat in the closet by the door (third hangar from the left) and then head to the kitchen for her daily inspection (exactly seven steps). She knew this because they had been roommates for six months. Taking a deep breath, she thought about what she would say to Brenda. She waited and watched from her spot on the couch.

A moment later, Brenda stepped into the kitchen and surveyed the scene. Anne watched her expression, watched her eyes focus on the sink, and watched her face harden when she saw the dishes piled high. Pointing to the dishes, Brenda said disappointedly, "I don't believe what I'm seeing. I thought we agreed to share the responsibilities. I thought it was your turn to clean the kitchen this week?"

"I haven't gotten to them yet," Anne replied. "I've been really busy. Relax. I've got all night." She walked into the kitchen and added her empty glass to the top of the pile.

Brenda fumed. "You know I'm having company tonight! Somehow I thought you would have done your share in the kitchen. If we want to remain roommates, things have to change."

The phone rang, and Anne darted to answer it.

Brenda said in the background, "Tell them to call back, we need to settle this now. I told you I'm having company soon."

Anne ignored Brenda's comment and continued to engage in conversation with a good friend of hers. "Did I ever tell you about the time when....."

Look carefully at the dialogue between these two characters. What do they say to each other? How is it said? What other clues from the author can you find in this passage to help you understand the cause of their conflict? List your observations below and then answer the questions that follow.

Your Observations:

Example: *I noticed that Ann was relaxing and watching TV when Brenda arrived.*

1. Why does Brenda get angry?
   a. Because Anne is unfriendly.
   b. Because she had a bad day at work.
   c. Because Anne didn't do the dishes.
   d. Because Anne is lazy.

2. Why didn't Anne do the dishes?
   a. Because she didn't have time to do them.
   b. Because she wanted to start a fight.
   c. Because she was too lazy.
   d. Because she wants Brenda to get a new roommate.

3. What does Anne do that shows she doesn't intend to shoulder her share of the responsibilities?
   a. She turns off the television.
   b. She begins to wash the dishes in the sink.
   c. She always helps around the house.
   d. She talks on the phone with a good friend.

Answers

1. **c.** Brenda's face "hardens" with anger when she sees the dishes in the sink. You can tell she expects the kitchen to be clean when she comes home. Anne waits for Brenda to begin her "daily inspection," and when she walks in, she looks around the kitchen as if she's inspecting it. Then she sees the dishes and her face hardens. She asks why the dishes are still in the sink. Further, she reminds Anne about the company she is expecting.

2. **b.** You can tell Anne is not worried about Brenda's reaction because she is lazily watching television instead of cleaning the kitchen. She knows Brenda is going to check the kitchen and that Brenda is going to be mad about the dishes when she sees them. As Anne waits, she thinks about what she is going to say to Brenda.

3. **d.** Anne's actions speak loudly. She answers the phone and discontinues a conversation that is important if the two of them intend to remain roommates.

FINDING IMPLIED EFFECTS

Just as writers can imply cause, they can also suggest effects. In the practice passage you just read, Anne clearly had a specific goal. She purposely decided not to do the dishes in an act of rebellion. Why? You know a little bit about Anne and Brenda from the passage. Use that knowledge to answer the following question. What do you think Anne was hoping to achieve? What effect do you think she was looking for?

1. That Brenda would do the dishes herself for once.
2. That Brenda would get herself a new roommate.
3. That Brenda would stop being so neat and so regimented.

How can you tell that 3 is the best answer? You have to look carefully at the passage. Anne says, "Relax. I've got all night." But, Brenda has her own priorities. She says she is expecting company. Anne responds by ignoring her and turning to a phone conversation.

The passage doesn't directly say so, but from these clues, you can conclude that Anne's personality is clearly more relaxed than Brenda's. That's why she didn't do the dishes and that's also why she gladly took a phone call.

But will she get the effect she hoped for? Take another look at the passage, paying close attention to the end. What do you think? Will Anne get her wish? Will Brenda change her ways? Why do you think so?

Most likely, Anne won't get her wish. How can you tell? The end of the passage offers a strong clue. Brenda clearly wants to resolve the situation, but she can't compete with the telephone and probably not with Anne's relaxed personality.

DETERMINING IMPLIED EFFECTS

In order to learn how to determine implied effects, take another look at Mr. Blank (the man who was robbed) and his building. Re-read the statements given by the building manager and Mr. Blank's neighbor and then use their statements to predict how the robbery will affect Mr. Blank and his building:

Building manager

This is the third robbery in our building this month. Each time, the thieves have gotten past building security with almost the entire contents of the victim's apartment. Yet each time, the security officers say they have seen nothing unusual.

Mr. Blank's neighbor

Well, Mr. Blank's a pretty carefree man. A few times I've knocked on his door and he just hollers, "Come in," and I just have to push the door open because it isn't locked. He often forgets things, too, like where he parked his car or where he put his keys. One time I found him in the hall searching through his bags because he couldn't find his keys, and it turned out the door was open anyway. Sometimes I wonder how he remembers to eat, let alone take care of his apartment.

Based on these two paragraphs, which of the following effects would be logical results (effects) of the robbery? Circle the correct answers.

1. Security will be tighter in the building from now on.

2. People moving furniture in and out of the building may be required to register with security.

3. The security officers will be fired.

4. Mr. Blank will get all of his belongings back.

5. Mr. Blank will be more careful about where he puts his keys.

6. Mr. Blank will get new locks on his door.

7. Mr. Blank will be sure to lock his door when he leaves.

8. Some tenants will leave the building.

Answers

Effects 1, 2, 5, 7, and 8 are logical predicted outcomes.

Effect 3 is not likely because it is too extreme; the building manager's statement does not suggest that he plans to fire the security guards. Rather, it suggests that he plans to look into the security problem.

There is nothing in either statement to suggest that effect 4 (that Mr. Blank will get his belongings back) is correct. In fact, there is no mention at all of his belongings.

Finally, because it is likely that Mr. Blank had left his door open on that day, there would be no need for him to get new locks on his door. Thus, number 6 is not a likely effect either.

SUMMARY

In reading, particularly in reading literature, as well as in real life, you often have to figure out what the causes of a particular event or situation might have been. The same is true of effects: both in reading and in life, you spend a lot of time trying to predict the outcomes of real or predicted actions or events. If you "read between the lines" without going too far beyond what the passage (or real-life event) actually contains, you can usually do a pretty good job of predicting these causes and effects.

Skill Building Until Next Time

- Observe people's behavior today. If you see people acting particularly happy, sad, or angry, or exhibiting some other strong emotion or behavior, see if you can find any clues as to the cause of their emotion or behavior. Are they reading a letter? Talking with someone? Waiting for something? *Why* are they reacting this way?
- Read a news article today that discusses a current event—an election, a train crash, or a political scandal, for example. What effects can you predict will come about as a result of this event? Try to come up with at least three predictions based on what you read.

EMOTIONAL VERSUS LOGICAL APPEALS

18

LESSON SUMMARY

Writers often appeal to your emotions to try to persuade you of something. But unless they also provide logical evidence to back up their claims, you have no *reason* to accept their argument as valid. This lesson helps you see how to distinguish between appeals to your emotions and appeals to your sense of reason.

Imagine that you are about to do something when someone runs up to you and says, "You can't do that!"

"Why not?" you ask.

"Because! You just can't, that's all."

Now, "Because!" is not likely to convince you that you shouldn't do what you were about to do, is it? Why not? Well, "Because!" does not provide you with a *reason* for not doing what you wanted to do. It is not, therefore, a very convincing argument.

THE DIFFERENCE BETWEEN LOGICAL AND EMOTIONAL APPEALS

When writers—and others—want to convince people of something—or to think a certain way—they generally rely on two means of persuasion: appealing to the reader's sense of logic, and appealing to the reader's emotions. It is important to be able to distinguish between these two types of appeal because when writers rely *only* on appeals to emotion they neglect to provide any real *evidence* for why you should believe what they say. Writers who rely solely on emotional appeals usually hope to get their readers so angry, scared, or excited that they will forget to look for reason or sense in the argument.

Unfortunately, many readers aren't aware of this strategy, so they may accept arguments that are unfounded, manipulative, or both. Political leaders who use the emotional strategy in speaking to crowds are called *demagogues*. Calling a leader a demagogue is no compliment since it means that he or she relies on prejudice and passion rather than clear thinking to persuade people of his or her position. Sound reasoning requires that you are able to look beyond emotional appeals to determine if there is any *logic* behind them.

Logical: according to reason; according to conclusions drawn from evidence or good common sense

Emotional: relating to emotions; arousing or exhibiting strong emotion

While it is true that an appeal to emotions can help *strengthen* an argument based in logic, an argument cannot be valid if it is based solely on emotional appeal.

DISTINGUISHING BETWEEN LOGICAL AND EMOTIONAL APPEALS

The best way to see the difference between logical and emotional appeals is to look at some examples. Actively read the passages that follow, trying to discern whether the author is appealing primarily to your sense of reason or to your emotions.

PRACTICE PASSAGE 1

The City Council of Ste. Jeanne should reject mandatory recycling. First of all, everyone knows that recycling doesn't really accomplish very much and that people who support it are mostly interested in making themselves *feel* better about the environment. They see more and more road construction and fewer and fewer trees and buy into the notion that sending bottles and cans to a recycling plant rather than a landfill will reverse the trend. Unfortunately, that notion is no more than wishful thinking.

Second, the proponents of mandatory recycling are the same people who supported the city's disastrous decision to require an increase in the number of public bus routes. After the mayor spent hundreds of thousands of dollars for the new buses and for street signs, bus shelters, and schedules, we all quickly learned that there was little to no interest in using public transportation among the people for whom the new routes were intended. Mandatory recycling would add yet another chapter to the book of wasteful government programs.

Finally, I'd like every citizen to answer this question in the privacy of his or her own heart: would the mandatory recycling law really influence behavior? Or would most people, in fact, go on doing what they are doing now? That is, wouldn't the recyclers keep on recycling and the people who throw their bottles and cans in the trash continue to do just that (only being a little bit more careful, burying the bottles inside "legal" trash such as pizza boxes and coffee filters)? Why should any of us be forced to be surreptitious about something so simple as throwing away a soft drink can? I urge both the council and the mayor to reject this misguided proposal.

Chances are that no matter how you *feel* about mandatory recycling programs, this passage provoked a reaction in you. Perhaps you found some of the writer's arguments convincing; perhaps they simply made you want to argue back. But take another look at the passage. Is there any appeal to your sense of logic here—reason, evidence, or common sense? Or is the author only appealing to your pre-existing ideas and feelings about environmentalism and government programs?

What Reasons Does the Writer Offer?

To help you see whether the writer's appeals are based on logic or emotion, break down his argument. The writer offers three different reasons for opposing the mandatory recycling proposal. Can you list them below?

1.

2.

3.

You probably noticed that each of the three paragraphs deals with a different reason that the writer opposes the mandatory recycling program. They are:

1. Recycling programs do not help the environment and people who support the mandatory recycling program do so simply in order to make themselves feel better about a declining environment.

2. The people who support mandatory recycling also supported a failed program to increase city bus routes.

3. A mandatory recycling program would not actually cause people who do not presently recycle to begin recycling.

Are the Appeals Logical?

Now the next step is to see if these reasons are *logical*. Does the author come to these conclusions based on reason, evidence, or common sense? If you look carefully, you will see that the answer is *no*. Each of the writer's arguments is based purely on emotion without any logic to support it.

Begin with the first reason: *Recycling programs do not help the environment and people who support the mandatory recycling program do so simply in order to make themselves feel better about a declining environment.* Is there any logic behind this argument? Is this statement based on evidence, such as poll data showing a link between feeling bad about the environment and supporting the program, or environmental reports showing that recycling doesn't improve the environment to any appreciable degree?

Regardless of whether you agree or disagree with this author, you can probably see that this argument is based only in emotion rather than in logic. The argument crumbles when you break it down. The author tries to blunt any skepticism about his argument by saying that "everyone knows" that recycling doesn't accomplish very much and that people support it mostly for selfish reasons. He states this as if it was an established fact but he fails to establish it with evidence. Even though many people may agree, no one can correctly claim that everyone knows this to be true—as presented, it is mere opinion. In fact, many people would argue in turn that recycling does a great deal to help clean up the environment. And if the writer cannot say for a fact that recycling doesn't work, how can he convincingly assert that people support it for selfish reasons?

Even without this flaw, the writer's argument is not logical because there is no evidence in this essay that the particular mandatory recycling program being discussed by the city council will not work. The author moves from stating his opposition to the program in the first sentence to a paragraph of unconvincing generalities about recycling programs in general.

The author's second argument is that *the people who support mandatory recycling also supported a failed program to increase city bus routes*. Is there any logic in this statement? No, not if we bear in mind that the point of the argument is the recycling program and not the bus route program. Readers who are sympathetic to the underlying message that many government programs are wasteful may get caught up in the emotion of their opinion and lose sight of the fact that the author is not even talking about the proposed mandatory recycling plan. The argument is designed to succeed by appealing to this underlying sympathetic response rather than by addressing the merits and demerits of the proposal being considered.

The third argument is that *a mandatory recycling program would not actually cause people who do not presently recycle to begin recycling*. Again, the author offers no evidence for his claim. Instead, he works on his readers' sense of shame about their own failure to comply with local ordinances or on their cynicism about whether their fellow citizens will comply with such rules. He doesn't offer evidence that people won't comply, or that the law enforcement authorities will be ineffective in forcing compliance, instead suggesting that the proposed program would be an undue burden, forcing good people to act "surreptitious," or stealthy, about everyday, innocent actions. Again, he avoids supporting his argument with logic, reason, or evidence.

PRACTICE PASSAGE 2

Now look at another argument for the same position. Notice how much more logical this essay is—whether you agree with the author or not—simply because the author gives explanations and evidence for his position rather than appealing solely to the readers' emotions.

The City Council of Ste. Jeanne should reject mandatory recycling. Although many good people support this idea, the proposal facing us is so deeply flawed that I believe their support is misplaced. The most glaring problem is that the mandatory recycling program proposed here would create at least as much pollution as it would eliminate. Our neighbors in Youngsville could testify to that: Greensleaves Recycling, the proposed contractor, got the recycling contract in Youngsville five years ago and their machinery spewed so much toxic gas out of its smokestacks that the city government stopped all recycling, mandatory or optional, for a solid year.

One of the biggest concerns people have is that the bottles and cans they throw away today will either accumulate in unsightly, unsanitary landfills or go up in smoke from an incinerator. But the fact of the matter is that new waste treatment facilities in nearby counties soon will eliminate most of the need for landfills and incinerators. By compacting unsorted trash into blocks comparable in hardness to concrete, the new facilities make it available for use in building foundations, dikes, and road construction. This form of "recycling" — not part of the present proposal — doesn't require us to collect the garbage in any new way because it doesn't matter whether the content is coffee grounds or juice bottles.

An argument in favor of the recycling proposal for which I have some sympathy is that mandatory recycling will raise people's awareness of our beautiful and fragile environment. Reflecting on this, however, I recalled our wonderful educational programs, both in the schools and in the mass media. Voluntary recycling is at an all-time high level of participation; both anglers and environmentalists are celebrating the recent re-opening of the Ste. Jeanne

Waterway to fishing; downtown Ste. Jeanne won the "Greening of the State" award just last year. Taken together, these facts suggest to me a populace already deeply engaged with environmental issues and now looking hard for new, well-conceived proposals to do even more. The present proposal simply doesn't measure up to our city's high standards.

You probably noticed immediately that this passage also gives three reasons for not supporting the mandatory recycling program—so the authors don't differ over whether or not to reject the proposed program. The two passages don't have as much in common in their style of argument, though, and that is our focus here. Let's take a closer look at Passage 2.

What Reasons Does the Writer Offer?

Break this argument down as you did the first one. Here are the reasons the author of Passage 2 provides in arguing that the mandatory recycling program should be rejected. Underneath each reason, make a note about the *logic* behind the reason; say what reasoning, evidence or common sense the author points to in support of the argument.

1. The proposed mandatory recycling program would cause as much pollution as it would eliminate.

2. New waste treatment facilities lessen the need for recycling programs.

3. The mandatory recycling program is not needed to raise people's awareness of the environment.

Are the Appeals Logical?

Whether you agree with the author or not, you can see that this is a much more effective argument because the writer uses logic and common sense in backing up what he has to say.

The first argument is supported in the following way:

-   The proposed contractor caused a great deal of pollution from smokestacks in a nearby city five years before.
-   The smokestack toxicity in the nearby city was so extensive that even voluntary recycling was halted for a year, meaning that even less recycling took place than before the mandatory recycling program began.

The second argument is supported by the following logic:

-   New waste treatment facilities allow all waste to be re-used without the need for sorting it into waste to be recycled and waste to be incinerated or put in a landfill, but the proposed plan does not involve these new facilities.

Finally, the third argument is supported this way:

-   The populace of Ste. Jeanne is already highly conscious of the environment, and benefit for educational programs in the schools and the mass media.
-   The high environment-consciousness of the people shows in (a) the high rate of voluntary recycling, (b) the celebrated re-opening of the Ste. Jeanne Waterway to fishing, and (c) the city's downtown winning a state environmental award the previous year.

MORE PRACTICE

Now that you've examined two brief essays—one that appeals to emotion and one that appeals to logic—see if you can correctly identify the approaches used by the writers of the following sentences. Look carefully for a sense of logic. If the writer is appealing to your emotions, is the author's argument also backed up by logic (common sense, reason, or evidence)? Write an E in the blank if it appeals *only* to your sense of emotion, and an L if it appeals to logic.

_____ 1. Gun control is wrong, and anyone who tries to tell me that I can't own a gun is stupid.

_____ 2. Gun control is wrong because it is a violation of our Constitutional right to bear arms.

_____ 3. Every state should have capital punishment. If everyone knows that the penalty for certain crimes is death, people are much less likely to commit those crimes.

_____ 4. We must have capital punishment. What if someone you love were killed; wouldn't you want the murderer to die?

_____ 5. Capital punishment is wrong; if we kill someone who is guilty of murder, we are guilty of the same crime as the criminal.

Answers

It should be clear that argument 1 is an appeal to emotion without any logic and that arguments 2, 3, and 5 use common sense, evidence, and reason. But argument 4 may have confused you a bit. The argument may seem reasonable, but it does not address *why* the murderer should die rather than, say, spend a lifetime in jail. Most of us might indeed wish death upon someone who murdered someone we love, but that is because we are deeply hurt by the loss of our loved one. Thus, this argument appeals to our emotions.

SUMMARY

Looking for appeals to logic will make you a more critical reader and thinker. And once you learn to read between the lines in an argument (to look behind emotional appeals for some sort of logical support), you'll have more confidence as a reader and be a better judge of the arguments that you hear and read.

Skill Building Until Next Time

- Listen carefully to how people around you try to convince you (or others) when they want you to think or act a certain way. For example, if a friend wants you to try a new place for lunch, how does he or she try to convince you: with appeals to your sense of logic ("The food is great—and so are the prices!") or to your emotions ("What, are you afraid to try something new?")? If your boss asks you to work overtime, does he or she appeal to your sense of logic ("You'll make lots of extra money") or to your emotions ("I could really, really use your help")? See which arguments you find most convincing and why.

- Read an editorial from the Opinion-Editorial page of your local newspaper. Look at how the writer supports his or her argument. Is the editiorial convincing? Why? What reasons or evidence does it use to support its position?

L·E·S·S·O·N
FINDING MEANING IN LITERATURE
19

LESSON SUMMARY

Lots of people are scared of reading literature—stories, poems, and plays—especially if they have to answer questions about it, as in a test situation. But now that you know so much about finding an implied main idea, you can also find the *theme,* or main idea, of a work of literature. This lesson works with poetry to show you how to do it.

h no! Not the "L" word!

Yes, it's time to talk about *literature.* Like many people, you may be intimidated by this ten-letter word. This is quite natural; after all, in literature (novels, poems, stories, and plays), the writers don't come right out and tell us what they mean. But, just as you were able to find the implied main idea in a passage where there was no topic sentence, you can look for clues the author has left behind to find the *theme* (the main idea) in any work of literature. You simply need to read between the lines to find meaning.

You probably remember the word *theme* from your high school English courses. Maybe you remember it with some confusion and trepidation. It's not as complicated as you might think.

You've spent a lot of time finding the main idea of a piece of writing. Finding the theme of a work of literature is similar to finding the main idea of a paragraph. Just as a main idea is more than the *subject* of a paragraph or passage, the theme of a work of literature is also more than just its subject: It is what the text says *about* that subject. Theme, in other words, is the overall message or idea that a work of literature conveys. For example, you can probably figure out from the title that the *subject* of John Donne's poem "Death Be Not Proud" is death. However, the *theme* is not merely "death," but what the poem says *about* death, which happens to be that death is a gift if one believes in God.

There isn't room in this short lesson to look at theme in a short story, novel, or play. So this lesson will introduce you to a few poems. But don't be frightened: Reading poetry is really just like reading anything else. You just have to read a little more carefully and rely a little more on your sense of observation. You find theme in poetry the same way you do in other kinds of writing: by looking for clues in what happens and in the words the writer uses to describe what happens.

HOW ACTION CONVEYS THEME

First, look at an example of how the action of a poem—what happens in it—leads you to understand the theme.

PRACTICE PASSAGE 1

Read the following poem by William Blake from his book *Songs of Experience*, published in 1794. Read it out loud, because poetry is meant to be *heard* as well as read. Then read it again with your pen in hand: Read actively, making your observations and comments in the margins. Then answer the questions that follow.

A Poison Tree

I was angry with my friend;
I told my wrath, my wrath did end.   wrath = anger
I was angry with my foe: foe = enemy
I told it not, my wrath did grow.

And I water'd it in fears,
Night & morning with my tears;
And I sunned it with smiles,
And with soft deceitful wiles.   wiles = trickery, deceit

And it grew both day and night,
Till it bore an apple bright;
And my foe beheld it shine,
And he knew that it was mine.

And into my garden stole
When the night had veil'd the pole: veiled = concealed
In the morning glad I see
My foe outstretch'd beneath the tree.

What Happened?

To understand the author's theme, you need to look carefully at what happened, and why. Look at each of the four stanzas (a stanza is a poetic "paragraph"; each stanza in this poem is four lines long) to track the action.

What happens in the first stanza?

1. The speaker was angry with
   a. a friend
   b. a foe
   c. his friend and his foe

2. How did the speaker handle his anger toward his friend?
   a. He told his friend about it and it went away.
   b. He kept it to himself and it grew.
   c. He kept it to himself and it went away.

3. How did the speaker handle his anger toward his foe?
   a. He told his friend about it and it went away.
   b. He kept it to himself and it grew.
   c. He kept it to himself and it went away.

You probably figured out the answers without too much trouble: **1. c, 2. a, 3. b.**

Now look at the second stanza. The key to understanding this stanza is knowing what "it" refers to. Reread the first and second stanzas carefully in order to answer the next question.

4. "It" refers to
   a. tears
   b. smiles
   c. wrath

"Wrath" is the last thing mentioned in the first stanza, so it follows that "wrath" is what "it" refers to.

The second stanza tells us that the speaker "water'd" it (his wrath) with fears and "sunned" it with smiles and wiles. How can this be? Can you literally water and sun your anger? No, but the speaker is not being literal here. Instead, he is using figurative language. Like the similes we saw earlier about Mr. B, comparing his eyes to knives and his mustache to Hitler's, this stanza uses a *metaphor*—a comparison that doesn't use the words *like* or *as*—to compare the speaker's wrath to something that grows with water and sun. Now, given these clues (and the best clue of all, the title of the

poem), to what exactly is the speaker comparing his wrath?

5. The speaker compares his wrath to
   a. a flower
   b. a tree
   c. the sun

The answer, of course, is **b**, a tree. The title gives this away. Also, a tree is the only plant that could bear "an apple bright," as in the third stanza.

What else happens in the third stanza?

6. In the third stanza, the foe
   a. grows his own apple
   b. shines the speaker's apple
   c. sees the speaker's apple

The answer is **c**, the foe sees the speaker's apple ("my foe beheld it shine").

Finally, what happens in the fourth stanza? This stanza is somewhat trickier than the others, because in this stanza, something happens that is not directly stated. You know that the foe sneaks into the speaker's garden ("And into my garden stole"), but what else happens?

The poem doesn't exactly tell you, but you can guess. The speaker had an apple; you know that this apple grew on a tree and that this tree is a metaphor for the speaker's anger. You also know that the poem is called "A Poison Tree." You read in the fourth stanza that, in the morning, the speaker finds his foe "outstretch'd beneath the tree." What can you conclude?

7. At the end of the fourth stanza, the foe
   a. is waiting to ambush the speaker and kill him with the apple
   b. has been killed by the apple he stole because it was poisonous
   c. is waiting to share the apple with the speaker

Which answer do your clues add up to? The only one that can be correct is **b**. The speaker was angry; the tree (and so the apple) was poisonous. You know that the foe, seeing the apple, snuck into the speaker's garden. Apparently he ate the apple, because now he's "outstretch'd beneath the tree." You also know that the speaker is "glad" to see his foe outstretched this way—he's glad to see him dead.

What Does It Mean?

Okay, so that's what happened in the poem. But what does it all mean?

Look again at the action. What the speaker *did* was to tell his friend about his wrath. What the speaker *didn't* do was to tell his enemy about his wrath. The results of the speaker's action and his inaction are your clues to the meaning of the poem as a whole, its theme.

8. Which of the following best summarizes the theme of the poem?
   a. Don't steal; it can kill you.
   b. Choose your enemies carefully.
   c. If you don't talk about your anger, it can be deadly.

Before you go any further, think about your answer again. Like a main idea, a theme must be general enough to encompass the whole work, not just a piece of it. Does the answer you chose encompass the whole poem and not just part of it?

You should have chosen answer **c**, for this is the idea that sums up the message or "lesson" of the poem. In the first two lines, the speaker's wrath for his friend vanished when he talked about it, but he did not talk about his wrath for his enemy. Instead, he let it grow until it was poisonous and deadly.

HOW LANGUAGE CONVEYS EMOTION

In addition to conveying a theme, poems also often use language to create a powerful image or emotion. After looking at how poets use language to convey an emotion or a picture, you'll be ready to put your understanding of the action and the language together to understand the meaning of a poem.

PRACTICE PASSAGE 2

Take a look at the following poem by the British poet Alfred, Lord Tennyson, as an example of how language can convey a strong feeling by conveying an image or picture. Read "The Eagle" twice out loud—remember, poetry is meant to be heard, not just seen. Then mark it up and write your observations in the margin.

The Eagle

He clasps the crag with crooked hands;   *crag = steep*
Close to the sun in lonely lands,   *or rugged rock*
Ringed with the azure world, he stands.   *azure = sky blue*

The wrinkled sea beneath him crawls;
He watches from his mountain walls,
And like a thunderbolt he falls.

The Sound of Words

What did you notice about the language in this poem? Did you notice the rhyme in each stanza—*hands, lands, stands* and *crawls, walls, falls*? Did you notice the repetition of the "k" sound in *c*lasps, *c*rag, and *c*rooked? This repetition of sounds (especially at the beginning of words) is called *alliteration*.

9. Which other line of this poem uses alliteration?
   a. line 2
   b. line 3
   c. line 6

The answer is line 2, which repeats the *l* sound in "*l*onely *l*ands."

Picture Language

You may have noticed another poetic device at work in this poem. In line 1, the poet tells us that the eagle ("he") "clasps" the rock "with crooked hands." Do eagles have hands? No, they do not; but Tennyson gives the eagle human characteristics. When an animal is given human characteristics, or when a inanimate thing (like a rock, for example) is given animate characteristics (human or animal), it is called *personification*.

10. Which other line of this poem uses personification?
   a. line 2
   b. line 4
   c. line 6

The other example of personification is found in line 4, where the sea "crawls" like a baby or a turtle.

Here's a memory test:

11. Line 6, "And like a thunderbolt he falls," uses which of the following poetic devices?
   a. personification
   b. simile
   c. irony

This line uses **b**, a simile that compares the eagle to a thunderbolt. What is the effect of this comparison?

12. The comparison of the eagle to a thunderbolt makes the reader think of the eagle as
   a. a weak, timid creature
   b. an unpredictable creature
   c. a powerful, fast creature

Like all good similes, this comparison creates a vivid image that not only helps us actually picture the eagle's flight but also tells us *something about* the eagle by comparing it to the incredible force of nature that is lightning. The eagle, this simile suggests, is as powerful, as fast, as dangerous—and as impossible to catch—as a thunderbolt. We should, in short, be as awed by the eagle as we are by lightning—and that feeling, more than an idea we might call a theme, is what this poem is all about.

ACTION + LANGUAGE = THEME

In the final poem for today, by the American poet Stephen Crane, see if you can determine the theme of the poem by looking at both the action of the poem and its language (diction, style, and tone). As before, begin by reading the poem carefully, first out loud and then with pen in hand.

PRACTICE PASSAGE 3

A Man Said to the Universe

A man said to the universe:
"Sir, I exist!"
"However," replied the universe,
"The fact has not created in me
A sense of obligation."

13. Which sentence best summarizes the theme of this poem?
   a. The universe is too big for humanity.
   b. The universe is indifferent to humanity.
   c. Humanity has an obligation to the universe.

The best answer is **b**, "The universe is indifferent to humanity." This idea is conveyed in part by the action of the poem: what the man says to the universe and the universe's reply. But the universe's indifference is also reflected in the language of the poem.

14. Which of the following best describes the tone of this poem?
   a. warm, caring
   b. hot, angry
   c. cold, formal

The words of this poem—especially "sir," "fact," and "sense of obligation"—are cold, formal words that reflect the way the universe feels about man: indifferent. There is no sense of intimacy, no relationship, no warmth in these words. The poet's diction and style help to reveal the theme of the poem.

SUMMARY

Reading poetry wasn't so bad after all, was it? If you are an active reader who is sensitive to the language used by the poet, you can use the clues the poet gives you to help you enjoy the pictures and emotions created through words and understand the poem's theme. And if you can do this for poems, you can certainly do it for stories, novels, and plays as well.

Skill Building Until Next Time
- Read a poem on your own today. See if you can read between the lines to determine its theme.
- Read a short story today. Apply the techniques you used to determine the theme in a poem to determine the theme of the story.

L·E·S·S·O·N 20

DRAWING CONCLUSIONS: PUTTING IT ALL TOGETHER

LESSON SUMMARY

This lesson wraps up your study of reading comprehension by reviewing everything you've learned so far.

ou're almost at the end of this book. If you've been doing a lesson every weekday, you've spent a month building your reading skills. Congratulations! This lesson uses a longer passage than the ones you've read so far to give you a chance to practice all the skills you've learned. Here's a quick review of what you've learned since the last review lesson:

- **Lesson 16: Finding an implied main idea.** You practiced looking for clues in structure, language, and style, as well as the facts of the passage, to determine the main idea.
- **Lesson 17: Understanding implied causes and effects.** You learned to "read between the lines" to determine causes and make predictions about effects.
- **Lesson 18: Emotional and logical appeals.** You learned that arguments that appeal to readers' emotions need to be supported by logic as well in order to be convincing.
- **Lesson 19: Finding the theme in literature.** You used your detective skills to find the main idea implied by the structure, language, style, and action in a work of literature.

If any of these terms or strategies sound unfamiliar to you, STOP. Please take a few minutes to review whatever lesson is unclear.

PRACTICE

Today, you'll practice the skills listed above in combination with skills covered earlier in this book:

- Finding the facts
- Determining the main idea
- Determining the meaning of unfamiliar words
- Distinguishing between fact and opinion
- Chronological order
- Order of importance
- Cause and effect
- Comparison and contrast
- Point of view
- Diction
- Language and style
- Tone

If this seems like a monumental task, don't worry: it isn't. You've already mastered some of these skills and should be very comfortable with the others. In fact, you will probably be surprised at how easy you find this exercise to be.

PRACTICE PASSAGE

Are you ready? Read the following essay. Remember, read actively and make observations in the space provided on the next page. Then answer the questions that follow. This will give you a chance to see how well your reading skills are coming along.

Although many companies offer tuition reimbursement, most companies only reimburse employ-ees for classes that are relevant to their position. This is a very limiting policy. A company that reimburses employees for all college credit courses—whether job related or not—offers a service not only to the employees, but to the entire company.

One good reason for giving employees unconditional tuition reimbursement is that it shows the company's dedication to its employees. In today's economy, where job security is a thing of the past and employees feel more and more expendable, it is important for a company to demonstrate to its employees that it cares. The best way to do this is with concrete investments in them.

In turn, this dedication to the betterment of company employees will create greater employee loyalty. A company that puts out funds to pay for the education of its employees will get its money back by having employees stay with the company longer. It will reduce employee turnover, because even employees who don't take advantage of the tuition reimbursement program will be more loyal to their company just knowing that their company cares enough to pay for their education.

Most importantly, the company that has an unrestricted tuition reimbursement program will have higher quality employees. Although these companies do indeed run the risk of losing money on employees who go on to another job in a different company as soon as they get their degree, more often than not, the employee will stay with the company. And even if employees do leave after graduation, it generally takes several years to complete any degree program. Thus, even if the employee leaves upon graduating, throughout those years the employer will have a more sophisticated, more intelligent, and, therefore, more valuable and productive employee. And, if the employee stays, that education will doubly benefit the company: Not only is the employee more educated, but now that employee can be promoted so the company doesn't have to fill a high-level vacancy from the outside. Open positions can be filled by people who already know the company well.

Though unconditional tuition reimbursement requires a significant investment on the employer's part, it is perhaps one of the wisest investments a company can make.

Your Observations

Record your observations about the passage in the space below.

Questions

1. According to the passage, unconditional tuition reimbursement is good for which of the following reasons?
   a. Employees get a cheaper education.
   b. Employees become more valuable.
   c. Employees can find better jobs.

2. How, according to the passage, will unconditional tuition reimbursement reduce employee turnover?
   a. by making employees more loyal
   b. by paying employees more money
   c. by promoting education

3. The first sentence of the passage, "Although many companies offer tuition reimbursement, most companies only reimburse employees for classes that are relevant to their position," is
   a. fact
   b. opinion

4. The second sentence of the passage, "This is a very limiting policy," is
   a. fact
   b. opinion

5. This passage is organized according to which of the following strategies? (Mark all that apply.)
   a. chronological order
   b. order of importance
   c. cause and effect
   d. compare and contrast

6. The point of view used in this passage is the
   a. first person point of view
   b. second person point of view
   c. third person point of view

7. The writer most likely chose this point of view because
   a. the writer is describing a personal experience
   b. it enables readers to identify with the situation
   c. its objectivity encourages the reader to take the writer's ideas seriously

8. The writer most likely uses the word *wisest* in the last sentence, rather than words such as *profitable, practical,* or *beneficial,* because
   a. wisdom is associated with education, the subject of the essay
   b. the writer trying to appeal to people who are already highly educated

9. Which of the following words best describes the tone of this essay?
   a. playful
   b. optimistic
   c. insincere

10. The passage suggests that, compared to employees of companies that offer unconditional tuition reimbursement, employees of companies that do not offer this benefit are
    a. less loyal
    b. more likely to be promoted
    c. not as smart

11. "Expendable" (paragraph 2) most nearly means
    a. expensive
    b. flexible
    c. replaceable

12. The writer appeals primarily to the reader's
    a. emotions
    b. sense of logic

13. The main idea of the passage is that
    a. companies should reimburse employees for work-related courses
    b. both companies and employees would benefit from unconditional tuition reimbursement
    c. companies should require their employees to take college courses

Answers

1. b. The idea that employees will become more valuable if they take courses is stated in the fourth paragraph: "Thus . . . the employer will have a more sophisticated, more intelligent, and therefore more valuable and productive employee."

2. a. The idea that employees will become more loyal is stated in the third paragraph: "A company that puts out funds to pay for the education of its employees will get its money back by having employees stay with the company longer. It will reduce employee turnover because even employees who don't take advantage of the tuition reimbursement program will be more loyal. . . ."

3. a. The sentence is a fact; you could verify it by surveying companies to find out about their tuition reimbursement policies.

4. b. The sentence is an opinion; it shows how the author feels about the policy.

5. b, c. The author lists the ways companies would benefit by having unconditional tuition reimbursement in order of importance from least to most important. The author also shows the positive effects unconditional reimbursement would have on the company.

6. c. There is no *I* or *you* here; the writer doesn't refer directly to herself or to the reader. Instead, everything is spoken of in the third person.

7. c. The writer most likely uses the third person point of view because it is objective, and her argument is more likely to be taken seriously. If she used the first person, readers might think she was an employee who wanted her employer to pay for her tuition, and she wouldn't be taken seriously.

8. a. By using a word associated with education, the writer stresses the importance of education for the company.

9. b. The passage describes only positive effects of unconditional reimbursement; there is scarcely a negative word.

10. a. If employees of companies that offer unconditional tuition reimbursement are more loyal to their companies (see the second and third paragraphs), it follows that other employees will be less

loyal because their company isn't showing enough dedication to their betterment.

11. c. Your best clue that *expendable* means *replaceable* is that the writer uses the word immediately after saying that job security is a thing of the past, so that workers don't feel they are important or valuable to a company that can fire them on a moment's notice.

12. b. There is common sense or reason behind each of the writer's arguments. Indeed, there are few, if any, emotional appeals in this passage.

13. b. This main idea is explicitly stated in the last sentence of the first paragraph (a good place to look for the main idea of a longer passage like this one) and repeated at the end of the passage.

How did you do? If you got all of the answers correct, congratulations! Good work. If you missed a few, you might want to take time to review the corresponding lessons.

If you missed:	Then study:
Question 1	Lesson 1
Question 2	Lesson 1
Question 3	Lesson 4
Question 4	Lesson 4
Question 5	Lessons 6–10
Question 6	Lesson 11
Question 7	Lesson 11
Question 8	Lesson 12
Question 9	Lesson 14
Question 10	Lessons 16 and 17
Question 11	Lesson 3
Question 12	Lesson 18
Question 13	Lessons 2 and 16

CONGRATULATIONS!

You've completed 20 lessons and have seen your reading skills increase. If you're preparing for a standardized test, you should check out Appendix A, which provides tips on how to prepare and what to do during the test. And don't forget Appendix B, which gives suggestions for how to continue to improve your reading skills, along with a list of suggested books organized by subject categories.

Now it's time to reward yourself for a job well done. Buy yourself a good book and enjoy!

POST-TEST

Now that you've spent a good deal of time improving your reading comprehension, take this post-test to see how much you've learned. If you took the pretest at the beginning of this book, you have a good way to compare what you knew when you started the book with what you know now.

When you complete this test, grade yourself, and then compare your score with your score on the pretest. If your score now is much greater than your pretest score, congratulations—you've profited noticeably from your hard work. If your score shows little improvement, perhaps there are certain chapters you need to review. Do you notice a pattern to the types of questions you got wrong? Whatever you score on this post-test, keep this book around for review and to refer to when you need tips on how to read more efficiently.

There's an answer sheet you can use for filling in the correct answers on the next page. Or, if you prefer, simply circle the answer numbers in this book. If the book doesn't belong to you, write the numbers 1–50 on a piece of paper and record your answers there. Take as much time as you need to do this short test. When you finish, check your answers against the answer key that follows this test. Each answer tells you which lesson of this book teaches you about the reading strategy in that question.

1.	ⓐ	ⓑ	ⓒ	ⓓ
2.	ⓐ	ⓑ	ⓒ	ⓓ
3.	ⓐ	ⓑ	ⓒ	ⓓ
4.	ⓐ	ⓑ	ⓒ	ⓓ
5.	ⓐ	ⓑ	ⓒ	ⓓ
6.	ⓐ	ⓑ	ⓒ	ⓓ
7.	ⓐ	ⓑ	ⓒ	ⓓ
8.	ⓐ	ⓑ	ⓒ	ⓓ
9.	ⓐ	ⓑ	ⓒ	ⓓ
10.	ⓐ	ⓑ	ⓒ	ⓓ
11.	ⓐ	ⓑ	ⓒ	ⓓ
12.	ⓐ	ⓑ	ⓒ	ⓓ
13.	ⓐ	ⓑ	ⓒ	ⓓ
14.	ⓐ	ⓑ	ⓒ	ⓓ
15.	ⓐ	ⓑ	ⓒ	ⓓ
16.	ⓐ	ⓑ	ⓒ	ⓓ
17.	ⓐ	ⓑ	ⓒ	ⓓ
18.	ⓐ	ⓑ	ⓒ	ⓓ
19.	ⓐ	ⓑ	ⓒ	ⓓ
20.	ⓐ	ⓑ	ⓒ	ⓓ

21.	ⓐ	ⓑ	ⓒ	ⓓ
22.	ⓐ	ⓑ	ⓒ	ⓓ
23.	ⓐ	ⓑ	ⓒ	ⓓ
24.	ⓐ	ⓑ	ⓒ	ⓓ
25.	ⓐ	ⓑ	ⓒ	ⓓ
26.	ⓐ	ⓑ	ⓒ	ⓓ
27.	ⓐ	ⓑ	ⓒ	ⓓ
28.	ⓐ	ⓑ	ⓒ	ⓓ
29.	ⓐ	ⓑ	ⓒ	ⓓ
30.	ⓐ	ⓑ	ⓒ	ⓓ
31.	ⓐ	ⓑ	ⓒ	ⓓ
32.	ⓐ	ⓑ	ⓒ	ⓓ
33.	ⓐ	ⓑ	ⓒ	ⓓ
34.	ⓐ	ⓑ	ⓒ	ⓓ
35.	ⓐ	ⓑ	ⓒ	ⓓ
36.	ⓐ	ⓑ	ⓒ	ⓓ
37.	ⓐ	ⓑ	ⓒ	ⓓ
38.	ⓐ	ⓑ	ⓒ	ⓓ
39.	ⓐ	ⓑ	ⓒ	ⓓ
40.	ⓐ	ⓑ	ⓒ	ⓓ

41.	ⓐ	ⓑ	ⓒ	ⓓ
42.	ⓐ	ⓑ	ⓒ	ⓓ
43.	ⓐ	ⓑ	ⓒ	ⓓ
44.	ⓐ	ⓑ	ⓒ	ⓓ
45.	ⓐ	ⓑ	ⓒ	ⓓ
46.	ⓐ	ⓑ	ⓒ	ⓓ
47.	ⓐ	ⓑ	ⓒ	ⓓ
48.	ⓐ	ⓑ	ⓒ	ⓓ
49.	ⓐ	ⓑ	ⓒ	ⓓ
50.	ⓐ	ⓑ	ⓒ	ⓓ

POST-TEST

The post-test consists of a series of reading passages with questions that follow to test your comprehension.

Statement by Senator Alan Cranston before the Senate Energy and Natural Resources Committee Subcommittee on Public Lands, National Parks and Forests in support of Senate Bill 7, the California Desert Protection Act, July 21, 1987 (excerpt)

Mr. Chairman, last April and May I made two trips to the California Desert with a group of naturalists, environmentalists, and scientists to look at some of the areas described in our legislation. We camped out on the desert floor. We hiked mountains. We trekked up and through narrow desert wilderness canyons. We found snakes, lizards, and other animals on huge, wild sand dunes. We looked at recreational sites for ORVs—dune buggies, ATVs, and motorcycles. We saw scores of flowers and plants, including an 11,000 year-old creosote bush which may be the oldest living organism on the planet Earth. We drove hundreds of miles over dirt and paved roads through Death Valley and Joshua Tree National Monuments. We flew over huge mining operations, water projects, military installations, and miles of farming and ranching lands. We held lizards in our hands and saw nighttime skies of incredible beauty and the myriad stars of endless galaxies.

One sunset we climbed the Eureka Dunes, looming, awesome sand structures that are a miniature ecosystem of incredible complexity. The dunes are surrounded by towering mountain ranges of rugged, stark, and massive igneous rocks whose antiquity and structure bespoke of long-ago geological eons.

Climbing the 8,500 foot Last Chance mountain peak, we saw a sweeping, 360-degree view, the snow-capped Sierra Nevada in the west and, far to the south, Death Valley sink, 280 feet below sea level. The awesome presence of overwhelming time and force surround you in the desert. There is an immense, almost incomprehensible beauty there that attracts people from all over the world, totaling some 16 million visitors a year.

The desert is a land of many uses and many resources. And it is vast enough to support the many varied demands being made upon it—by recreationists, campers, hikers, tourists, military, residents, energy developers, miners, rockhounds, hunters, ranchers, naturalists, scientists, and educators. The desert *can* support all those diverse interests *provided only* that the demands made upon it are in concert with the ecological and economic realities of the region.

… I've made other trips to the desert, but this time I came away more determined than ever to help conserve, protect and manage these vast natural resources for the greatest number of people and for the greatest good, not just of California, but the nation as a whole; and not just for the immediate gratification of a few, but for the millions in future generations who follow in our footsteps.

Mr. Chairman, this legislation is necessary because of the breach of trust by Secretary Hodel—"Mr. Environment Buster"—in failing to protect the desert. His opposition to our bill is unfortunate but not surprising, considering his record over the past 2-1/2 years. From the mountains to the deserts, from the oceans to the ozone, Hodel has aided and abetted a creeping destruction, degradation and devastation of our environment. Hodel closes his eyes to strip mining violations in Kentucky, ignores the problems of acid rain in New England and Canada, pushes oil exploration and drilling in protected sanctuaries of Alaska, condones below-rim tourist flights through the Grand Canyon, and encourages oil companies to rape the beauty and the resources of coasts on both sides of our continent, from California to Massachusetts.

1. In the opening paragraph, Senator Cranston includes several short sentences beginning with the word "we." What is the most likely purpose of this repeated sentence structure?
   a. to emphasize on the Senator's willingness to exert himself
   b. to emphasize how comprehensive the study was
   c. to emphasize the rugged physical nature of the desert landscape
   d. to contrast the natural beauty of the desert with the scars left on the terrain by humans

2. Cranston's description of his visit to the desert is arranged
   a. chronologically, in the order desert sites were visited
   b. chronologically, with more ancient geological features preceding more recent developments
   c. by importance, with more significant features listed first
   d. poetically, according to the impact of the language

3. Which of the following things is NOT included in Senator Cranston's list of things he saw in the desert?
   a. Death Valley
   b. recreational areas
   c. military installations
   d. Devil's Playground sand dunes

4. Senator Cranston's primary concern is that
   a. the desert be preserved
   b. private enterprise continue to have access to the desert's resources
   c. tourists and other recreationists be given greater access to the desert
   d. access to the desert be cut off entirely so that it can have a chance to heal itself

5. In describing the actions of Secretary of the Interior Hodel, Cranston creates a portrait of a man who
   a. fails to stand up to the misguided demands of the public at large
   b. profits financially from the abuse of public resources
   c. allows and even promotes the ruin of the natural areas under his care
   d. has a greater interest in protecting forests and seashores than in protecting the desert

6. By calling Secretary Hodel "Mr. Environment Buster," Senator Cranston is
   a. using a time-honored form of political argument that dignifies his own position on the issues
   b. resorting to name calling, a lower form of argument that is likely to alienate his political adversaries
   c. making an objective, unemotional assertion based on his observations of the Secretary's practices
   d. merely quoting what others say about the Secretary and thereby distancing himself from the opinion

7. Throughout the passage on Secretary Hodel, Cranston uses all of the following verbs to express his disapproval of the Secretary's practices. Which most heatedly conveys this negative opinion?
   a. to aid and abet
   b. to condone
   c. to rape
   d. to ignore

Summaries of Three Recent Studies on Smoking
The U.S. Center for Disease Control (CDC)
(excerpt)

The first article, State-Specific Prevalence of Cigarette Smoking—United States, 1995, represents the first compilation of adult smoking prevalence rates reported in compliance with the recommendation unanimously voted on by the Council of State and Territorial Epidemiologists to add prevalence of cigarette smoking to the list of conditions designated as reportable by states to the CDC. This study shows more than a twofold variation in state-specific smoking rates. Other findings of the study include the prevalence of current cigarette smoking ranged from 13.2% in Utah to 27.8% in Kentucky. This wide variation shows there is much room for progress in reducing tobacco use and improving tobacco control measures. Only Utah has achieved the national health objective for the year 2000 of reducing the prevalence of cigarette smoking among adults to no more than 15%; this objective has been nearly met in California. The percentage of smokers who smoke every day ranged from 79.7% in New Jersey to 92.9% in Oklahoma. The percentage of every-day smokers who had quit for at least one day in the past year ranged from 32.4% in Georgia to 59.4% in Hawaii.

The second article, *Cigarette Smoking Before and After an Excise Tax Increase and an Anti-Smoking Campaign—Massachusetts, 1990-1996,* shows that combining a cigarette tax hike with a statewide media campaign markedly reduced cigarette consumption in Massachusetts. Between 1992 and 1996, per capita cigarette consumption in Massachusetts fell more than three times as fast as in the 48 states not having such a program. Other findings of the study include between 1992, the year prior to implementation of the voters' petition, and 1996, per capita cigarette consumption declined 20 percent in Massachusetts compared with 16 percent in California, the only other state with a similar ballot initiative, and 6 percent in the other 48 states and the District of Columbia. In the period 1990–1992 to 1993–1995, adult smoking prevalence declined at similar rates in Massachusetts (2.2 percentage points) and California (2.7 percentage points) and by about 0.8 percentage points for 41 other states combined (where state-specific prevalence rates were available). The decline in per-capita cigarette consumption in Massachusetts between 1992 and 1996 cannot be attributed to purchases in neighboring states, particularly New Hampshire.

The third article, *Projected Smoking Related Deaths Among Youth—United States,* estimates that unless teen smoking rates are cut immediately, more than 5 million young people under age 18 will die from a smoking-related disease. These deaths could result in almost $200 billion in future health care costs and about 64 million years of life lost for the youth of this nation. The study also found more than 5 million children living today will die prematurely because of a decision they will make as adolescents—the decision to smoke cigarettes. One out of three young people (32 percent) who become regular smokers will die of a smoking-related disease. More than half (55 percent) of smokers continue to smoke up to one year before their death.

8. Applying the facts about tobacco-related deaths discussed in the last paragraph to the data on smoking rates in paragraph one, which of the following states is likely to have the lowest mortality rate from smoking in the future?
a. California
b. Utah
c. Kentucky
d. Hawaii

9. Which state has the highest percentage of smokers who smoke daily?
a. Oklahoma
b. New Jersey
c. Massachusetts
d. Georgia

10. "This wide variation shows there is much room for progress in reducing tobacco use and improving tobacco control measures." This sentence from paragraph one draws its conclusion from
a. statistics showing the differences in smoking rates between some states
b. a comparative study of anti-smoking efforts made in the various states
c. the change in smoking rates observed over the period under study
d. the increase in the number of young people using tobacco products

11. Look again at the sentence quoted in question 10. An alternative way of phrasing this argument would be to say "This wide variation shows that tobacco control measures have failed." What effect would this alternative wording have on readers?
a. It would reduce their confidence in the author.
b. It would make them question the data since the conclusion goes against logic.
c. It would make them look more favorably upon the efforts that have been made to date.
d. It would make them look less favorably upon the efforts that have been made to date.

12. What, according to the passage, is the relationship between smoking rates in Massachusetts and in California?
a. Both states have a low incidence of smoking fatalities.
b. Both states saw adult smoking rates decline by 2 percent or more.
c. Both states have reached the 15 percent smoking objective for year 2000.
d. These two states have the lowest percentages of people who smoke.

13. If a writer wished to rely on the statistics provided in this article to make an anti-smoking argument, what would the most likely conclusion be?
a. Tobacco use can be effectively reduced through excise taxes and anti-smoking campaigns.
b. Tobacco use cannot be effectively reduced through excise taxes and anti-smoking campaigns.
c. Tobacco use can be effectively reduced through excise taxes, but not through anti-smoking campaigns.
d. Tobacco use can be effectively reduced through anti-smoking campaigns, but not through excise taxes.

14. The final sentence of paragraph two states that "reduced smoking in Massachusetts cannot be attributed to purchases in neighboring states." This statement is presented as
   a. an opinion and has logic supporting it
   b. an opinion but has no logic supporting it
   c. a fact and has logic supporting it
   d. a fact but has no logic supporting it

15. "The study also found more than 5 million children living today will die prematurely because of a decision they will make as adolescents—the decision to smoke cigarettes." This idea from paragraph three could be also briefly stated as: "The study also found more than 5 million children will die prematurely because of a decision they will make as adolescents to smoke cigarettes." If the author wishes to discourage cigarette smoking, which alternative is best, and why?
   a. The first, because the more words that are devoted to an argument, the more likely it is to have an impact.
   b. The first, because the phrase "living today" underscores the tragedy, and because the repetition of the word "decision" drives home the choice involved.
   c. The second, because it is more direct and to the point.
   d. The second, because it makes the relationship clearer between the decision and death.

"The Weekly Visit"
(short story excerpt)

The requisite visit happened typically on sunny Saturdays, when my child spirits were at their highest and could be most diminished by the cramped interior of her house. My mother, accustomed to the bright, spacious farmhouse that was once Grandma's seemed no less susceptible to the gloom. She would set her jaw as Grandma described the many ailments attendant on age and would check her watch—an hour being the minimum she expected herself to withstand. Her barely contained impatience and my grandmother's crippling age radiated out around me. We were the women of the Carlson clan, each throbbing with agitation, like concentric, blinking circles on a radar screen.

I would sit at the white and red metal table with the pull-out leaves and built-in silverware drawer, cracking almonds. This was the one good thing at Grandma's house, the almonds, which she kept in a green Depression glass bowl. I would lift the lid carefully and try to set it down on the metal table quietly, then attempt to crack the nuts without scattering the shell crumbs. It was not good to draw attention to myself at Grandma Carlson's. Sounding angry, she would call to me in her croupy drawl. When I failed to understand her, she would reach out to me with her palsied, slick, wrinkled hand and shout, "Here!" She would be offering some of her horehound candy, which tasted like a cross between butterscotch and bitter sticks.

There was this lamentable air in the dim house with its itchy mohair furniture and its dark colors, an awareness—Grandma's—underlying the mentholatum, that her age scared her grandkids. I would yearn during the dutiful visit to get outside into the yard, where Grandma had transplanted a few flowers when she moved from the farm. But even the yard, with its overgrown hedges and rusted metal lawn chairs, seemed dreary. When I came back inside, light and air bursting in with me, Grandma, her hair up in a gray bun, would rock a little and smile. I would lean then against my mother's chair, Grandma's fond eyes peering at me, and whisper out of the corner of my mouth, "Mom, can we go?"

16. From the overall context of the passage, it is most likely that the word "lamentable" at the beginning of the third paragraph, means
a. laughable
b. sad
c. insane
d. inspired

17. Which of the following does the radar screen image underscore?
a. the narrator's absorption in gadgets and the modern world
b. the narrator's daydreaming nature
c. the narrator's uneasy sense of herself in the same lineage as her mother and grandmother
d. all of the above

18. In revising this story, the author is considering taking out the reference to "butterscotch and bitter sticks" and instead describing the candy as "bitter with a sweet under-taste." Which is better— the original or this alternative description—and why?
a. the original, because it leaves the actual taste up to the reader's imagination
b. the original, because it is more vivid and exact
c. the alternative, because it is more brief and to the point
d. the alternative, because it is more vivid and exact

19. Assume this piece is fiction and could have been written from any point of view. What would a switch to third person achieve?
a. Readers would be somewhat distanced from the narrator's feelings.
b. The author would have more latitude to express the narrator's feelings.
c. Readers would be more likely to identify with the feelings expressed.
d. The grandmother's feelings would become more apparent.

20. In a previous version of this story, the author described the garden as having "lush hedges and quaint metal chairs." Why is it more effective to describe the hedges as "overgrown" and the chairs as "rusted"?
a. These words add to the sense of age lingering over the place.
b. These words have a negative connotation, which mirrors the girl's feelings about the visits.
c. These words make the garden seem like less of an escape than the girl had hoped for.
d. All of the above reasons apply.

21. Which of the following accurately reflects the comparative attitudes of the characters in this excerpt?
a. The attitudes of the mother and the daughter are similar.
b. The attitudes of the grandmother and the mother are similar.
c. The attitudes of the grandmother and the granddaughter are similar.
d. The attitudes of the mother and the daughter are dissimilar.

The Wolf and the Crane

A wolf who had a bone stuck in his throat hired a crane, for a large sum, to put her head into his mouth and draw out the bone. When the crane had extracted the bone and demanded the promised payment, the wolf, grinning and grinding his teeth, exclaimed: "Why you have surely already had a sufficient recompense, in having been permitted to draw out your head in safety from the mouth and jaws of a wolf."

22. Following is a list of morals from this and other Aesop fables. Which one is the most likely companion to this fable?
    a. Self-help is the best help.
    b. The loiterer often blames delay on his more active friend.
    c. The greatest kindness will not bind the ungrateful.
    d. In serving the wicked, expect no reward.

Fly-Rights—A Consumer Guide to Air Travel
(excerpt)

If your reservations are booked far enough ahead of time, the airline may offer to mail your tickets to you. However, if you don't receive the tickets and the airline's records show that they mailed them, you may have to go through cumbersome lost-ticket procedures. It is safer to check the telephone directory for a conveniently located travel agency or airline ticket office and buy your tickets there.

As soon as you receive your ticket, check to make sure all the information on it is correct, especially the airports (if any of the cities have more than one) and the flight dates. Have any necessary corrections made immediately.

It's a good idea to reconfirm your reservations before you start your trip; flight schedules sometimes change. On international trips, most airlines require that you reconfirm your onward or return reservations at least 72 hours before each flight. If you don't, your reservations may be canceled.

Check your tickets as you board each flight to ensure that only the correct coupon has been removed by the airline agent.

23. Numbering the paragraphs 1 through 4 as they now appear, choose the option below that places them in chronological order.
    a. 2, 3, 4, 1
    b. 3, 1, 2, 4
    c. 3, 2, 1, 4
    d. 1, 2, 3, 4

24. Notice that this manual is written in the second person, employing the "you" pronoun. Considering the purpose of the manual, is this the best choice and why?
    a. Yes, because it avoids the necessity to choose between male and female pronouns.
    b. Yes, because the people who will be doing the traveling are addressed directly.
    c. No, because not all people travel by plane.
    d. No, because it makes readers unnecessarily uncomfortable to be addressed directly.

25. In paragraph one, as the passage appears above, why is it suggested that you buy your tickets from a "conveniently located" agency or office?

    a. because you can stop on your way to the airport to pick up your tickets

    b. because you can pick your tickets up rather than relying on the mail

    c. because the airlines themselves often make mistakes in issuing tickets

    d. because it is good to support local businesses

26. Which is a possible result of not following the advice offered in the first sentence of paragraph 2?

    a. You might fly into the right city, but the wrong airport.

    b. You might miss your flight, because the date was improperly recorded.

    c. You might not be allowed to board your flight because the name on the ticket doesn't match that on your ID

    d. Any of the above could happen as a result of not following the advice.

Bear Story

Campers Gene and Marie Marsden took pride in being good citizens when in the wild. While driving the three hundred miles from their home in Colorado to the Green River Lakes area of the Wind River Mountains in Wyoming, they instructed their children in the protocol they'd learned in the bear safety pamphlet put out by the Bridger-Teton Forest Service. The number-one rule was "Don't feed the bears!"—whether intentionally or not. Warning the kids not to go anywhere near a bear, the Marsdens had no problem with the intentional part, but the unintentional part was not as easy to avoid as they thought.

Mr. and Mrs. Marsden did their best to keep a tidy camp. While the bear manual had said to hang all food at least ten feet off the ground and four feet out from the trunk of a tree, they did what all the other people in the nearby public campground were doing and locked their food in their little utility trailer at night. Afraid that the scent of the bait might attract a bear, they even locked up Marie's fishing pole. It was always dark when they went to bed, but they perused the campsite with flashlights, making sure nothing was left out. Taking the recommended precaution of sleeping a hundred yards from where they cooked their food, they kept the car near their tents, unhitched from the trailer, which they left up at the other camp. Before going to bed each night, all of the Marsdens took off the clothes they had worn during the day while eating, replacing them with pajamas that they used only for sleeping. They were careful to lock the dirty laundry in the trailer also. As the pamphlet advised, they took no snacks into their tents.

Gene says he now regrets not having taken their dog into the tent at night, but they liked having him on guard. Small animals would often come sniffing around, and the dog would chase them back into the thickets, then return to the hollow he'd dug for himself in front of the children's tent. But on the night of the encounter, Spike would not stop barking, and Marie Marsden knew he must be sounding the alarm on something more dangerous and dauntless than a raccoon or squirrel. When she unzipped the tent and shined her flashlight in the direction of the cooking area, she saw Spike attempting to hold at bay a young grizzly bear.

They all managed to pile into the car, and with the kids sitting atop stuff sacks full of clothes and gear, they drove quickly down the trail, calling out the window to Spike and abandoning the cargo trailer to whatever fate the bear might have in store for it. Uncertain whether the bear was following or not, one of the children opened a door and loaded Spike up on the run. They drove to a pay phone twenty miles away and called a Fish and Game Department ranger, who identified the bear by the white ruff the Marsdens had seen around his neck. The authorities informed the Marsdens that the bear was a young, recently weaned male that they'd been keeping an eye on.

The next morning, the Marsdens heard helicopters circling over the mountain above them and wondered if it might have something to do with the bear. After spending the night in the public campground, they drove back to their site. Wandering the area in search of clues, Marie came to a halt below the tallest spruce. She slapped her head and shouted, "Oh no!"

"What is it?" Gene asked.

Marie pointed at the ground where Spike's dog food bowl lay upside down.

A week after their return home, the Marsdens read the headline in their local paper. "Bear Euthanized in Wind Rivers." According to the article, the Fish and Game Department had shot the young bear because, having been rewarded for invading a human campsite, it would likely do so again.

The Marsdens knew they had been lucky in the encounter, yet much to their shame and sadness, they also knew that the bear had not.

27. Which of the following statements is true?
   a. The Marsdens went camping in the Wind River Mountains of Wyoming.
   b. The pamphlet on camping in bear country was sent to the Marsdens by the Fish and Game Department.
   c. The Marsdens went camping in the Green River Lakes area near their hometown.
   d. All of the above statements are true.

28. Who does the author imply is mostly to blame in the bear's death?
   a. The Marsdens, because they were not careful enough.
   b. The bear, because he invaded a human camp.
   c. The Fish and Game authorities, because of poor communication with campers.
   d. The Forest Service, for putting out incomplete information.

29. In paragraph two, it can be determined from the context that the word "perused" means
   a. neglected
   b. cleaned
   c. studied
   d. hid

30. In paragraph three, it can be determined from the context that the word "dauntless" means
   a. stupid
   b. fearless
   c. clumsy
   d. spineless

31. This story is arranged
   a. like a news story, with the most important event told first
   b. in reverse chronological order, with the last event first
   c. in standard chronological order, with events told in the order they occurred
   d. in mixed, random order

32. What was the "reward" referred to in the next to last paragraph?
    a. the bear seeing the Marsdens run from him
    b. the bear receiving no punishment for disturbing humans
    c. the bear being able to stand off Spike
    d. the bear getting the dog food

33. The tone and style of this piece make it appropriate for which of the following types of publications?
    a. a scientific report on human-bear interaction
    b. a pamphlet on bear safety such as the one the Marsdens read
    c. a statistical study on bear fatalities in the Western mountains
    d. a human interest article in the Sunday magazine of a newspaper

A Plains Childhood

When I think of my family's history on the land, I experience a pang of regret. Unlike much of the arid West, where the land has gone virtually unchanged for centuries, my place of origin, western Kansas, has been torn up by agriculture. The flat plains, excellent soil, and sparse but just adequate rainfall permitted farming; therefore farming prevailed, and a good ninety percent of the original sod prairie is gone. The consequence, in human terms, is that our relationship to our place has always felt primarily mercantile. We used the land and denied, or held at bay, its effect on us. Yet from my earliest childhood, when most of the Kansas prairie was still intact, I've known that the land also had a romantic quality. I've felt moved by the expanse of it, enthralled by its size. I take pride in my identity as a plains daughter.

34. Which of the following is the most accurate restatement of the author's position?
    a. The presence of people has enriched the Plains habitat.
    b. Farming has improved the soil of the Plains.
    c. Farming has eroded the natural beauty of the Plains.
    d. Farming has chemically polluted the Plains.

35. The argument in this paragraph is based primarily on
    a. facts of history and statistical studies
    b. facts derived from the author's personal observations
    c. feelings the author has picked up from personal experience
    d. feelings passed down to the author by her ancestors

36. From context it can be determined that the word "mercantile" has something to do with
    a. practicality
    b. danger
    c. America
    d. spirituality

The coast of the State of Maine is one of the most irregular in the world. A straight line running from the southernmost coastal city to the northernmost coastal city would measure about 225 miles. If you followed the coastline between these points, you would travel more than ten times as far. This irregularity is the result of what is called a drowned coastline. The term comes from the glacial activity of the ice age. At that time, the whole area that is now Maine was part of a mountain range that towered above the sea. As the glacier descended, however, it expended enormous force on those mountains, and they sank into the sea.

As the mountains sank, ocean water charged over the lowest parts of the remaining land, forming a series of twisting inlets and lagoons of contorted grottos and nooks. The highest parts of the former mountain range, nearest the shore, remained as islands. Mt. Desert Island was one of the most famous of all the islands left behind by the glacier. Marine fossils found here were 225 feet above sea level indicating the level of the shoreline prior to the glacier.

The 2500 mile long rocky and jagged coastline of Maine keeps watch over nearly two thousand islands. Many of these islands are tiny and uninhabited, but many are home to thriving communities. Mt. Desert Island is one of the largest, most beautiful of the Maine coast islands. Measuring 16 miles by 12 miles, Mt. Desert was very nearly formed as two distinct islands. It is split almost in half by Somes Sound, a very deep and very narrow stretch of water seven miles long.

For years, Mt. Desert Island, particularly its major settlement, Bar Harbor, afforded summer homes for the wealthy. Recently though, Bar Harbor has become a burgeoning arts community as well. But, the best part of the island is the unspoiled forest land known as Acadia National Park. Since the island sits on the boundary line between the temperate and sub-Arctic zones, the island supports the flora and fauna of both zones as well as beach, inland, and alpine plants. It also lies in a major bird migration lane and is a resting spot for many birds.

The establishment of Acadia National Park in 1916 means that this natural monument will be preserved and that it will be available to all people, not just the wealthy. Visitors to Acadia may receive nature instruction from the park naturalists as well as enjoy camping, hiking, cycling, and boating. Or they may choose to spend time at the archeological museum learning about the Stone Age inhabitants of the island.

The best view on Mt. Desert Island is from the top of Cadillac Mountain. This mountain rises fifteen hundred and thirty-two feet, making it the highest mountain on the Atlantic seaboard. From the summit, you can gaze back toward the mainland or out over the Atlantic Ocean and contemplate the beauty created by a retreating glacier.

37. Which of the following lists of topics best outlines the information in the selection?

   a. — Ice-age glacial activity
      — The Islands of Casco Bay
      — Formation of Cadillac Mountain
      — Summer residents of Mt. Desert Island

   b. — Formation of a drowned coastline
      — The topography of Mt. Desert Island
      — The environment of Mt. Desert Island
      — Tourist attractions on Mt. Desert Island

   c. — Mapping the Maine coastline
      — The arts community at Bar Harbor
      — History of the National Park system
      — Climbing Cadillac Mountain

   d. — The effect of glaciers on small islands
      — Stone-age dwellers on Mt. Desert Island
      — The importance of bio-diversity
      — Hiking in Acadia National Park

38. Which of the following statements best expresses the main idea of paragraph four of the selection?

   a. The wealthy residents of Mt. Desert Island selfishly kept it to themselves.
   b. Acadia National Park is one of the smallest of the national parks.
   c. On Mt. Desert Island, there is great tension between the year-round residents and the summer tourists.
   d. Due to its location and environment, Mt. Desert Island supports an incredibly diverse animal and plant life.

39. According to the selection, the large number of small islands along the coast of Maine are the result of

   a. glaciers forcing a mountain range into the sea.
   b. Maine's location between the temperate and sub-Arctic zones.
   c. the irregularity of the Maine coast.
   d. the need for summer communities for wealthy tourists and artists.

40. The content of paragraph five indicates that the writer believes that

   a. the continued existence of national parks is threatened by budget cuts.
   b. the best way to preserve the environment on Mt. Desert Island is to limit the number of visitors.
   c. national parks allow large numbers of people to visit and learn about interesting wilderness areas.
   d. Mt. Desert Island is the most interesting tourist attraction in Maine.

41. According to the selection, the coast of Maine is

   a. 2500 miles long.
   b. 3500 miles long.
   c. 225 miles long.
   d. 235 miles long.

42. What is the meaning of the underlined phrase flora and fauna in paragraph four of this passage?

   a. insects and plants
   b. plants and animals
   c. deer and coyote
   d. birds and beaches

The immune system is equal in complexity to the combined <u>intricacies</u> of the brain and nervous system. The success of the immune system in defending the body relies on a dynamic regulatory communications network consisting of millions and millions of cells. Organized into sets and subsets, these cells pass information back and forth like clouds of bees swarming around a hive. The result is a sensitive system of checks and balances that produces an immune response that is prompt, appropriate, effective and self-limiting.

At the heart of the immune system is the ability to distinguish between self and nonself. When immune defenders encounter cells or organisms carrying foreign or nonself molecules, the immune troops move quickly to eliminate the intruders. Virtually every body cell carries distinctive molecules that identify it as self. The body's immune defenses do not normally attack tissues that carry a self-marker. Rather, immune cells and other body cells coexist peaceably in a state known as self-tolerance. When a normally functioning immune system attacks a nonself molecule, the system has the ability to "remember" the specifics of the foreign body. Upon subsequent encounters with the same species of molecules, the immune system reacts accordingly. With the possible exception of antibodies passed during lactation, this so called immune system memory is not inherited. Despite the occurrence of a virus in your family, your immune system must "learn" from experience with the many millions of distinctive nonself molecules in the sea of microbes in which we live. Learning entails producing the appropriate molecules and cells to match up with and counteract each nonself invader.

Any substance capable of triggering an immune response is called an antigen. Antigens are not to be confused with allergens, which are most often harmless substances (such as ragweed pollen or cat hair) that provoke the immune system to set off the inappropriate and harmful response known as allergy. An antigen can be a virus, a bacterium, a fungus, a parasite, or even a portion or product of one of these organisms. Tissues or cells from another individual (except an identical twin, whose cells carry identical self-markers) also act as antigens; because the immune system recognizes transplanted tissues as foreign, it rejects them. The body will even reject nourishing proteins unless they are first broken down by the digestive system into their primary, non-antigenic building blocks. An antigen announces its foreignness by means of intricate and characteristic shapes called epitopes, which protrude from its surface. Most antigens, even the simplest microbes, carry several different kinds of epitopes on their surface; some may even carry several hundred. Some epitopes will be more effective than others at stimulating an immune response. Only in abnormal situations does the immune system wrongly identify self as nonself and execute a misdirected immune attack. The result can be a so-called autoimmune disease such as rheumatoid arthritis or systemic lupus erythematosis. The painful side effects of these diseases are caused by a person's immune system actually attacking itself.

43. What is the analogy used to describe the communications network among the cells in the immune system?
a. the immune system's memory
b. immune troops eliminating intruders
c. bees swarming around a hive
d. a sea of microbes

44. The immune cells and other cells in the body coexist peaceably in a state known as
a. equilibrium
b. self-tolerance
c. harmony
d. tolerance

45. What is the specific term for the substance capable of triggering an inappropriate or harmful immune response to a harmless substance such as ragweed pollen?
a. antigen
b. microbe
c. allergen
d. autoimmune disease

46. How do the cells in the immune system recognize an antigen as "foreign" or "non-self?"
a. through an allergic response
b. through blood type
c. through fine hairs protruding from the antigen surface
d. through characteristic shapes on the antigen surface

47. After you have had the chicken pox, your immune system will be able to do all of the following EXCEPT
a. prevent your offspring from infection by the chicken pox virus.
b. distinguish between your body cells and that of the chicken pox virus.
c. "remember" previous experiences with the chicken pox virus.
d. match up and counteract non-self molecules in the form of the chicken pox virus.

48. Which of the following best expresses the main idea of this passage?
a. An antigen is any substance that triggers an immune response.
b. The basic function of the immune system is to distinguish between self and non-self.
c. One of the immune system's primary functions is the allergic response.
d. The human body presents an opportune habitat for microbes.

49. Why would tissue transplanted from father to daughter have a greater risk of being detected as foreign than a tissue transplanted between identical twins?
a. The age of the twins' tissue would be the same, and therefore less likely to be rejected.
b. The identical twin's tissue would carry the same self-markers and would therefore be less likely to be rejected.
c. The difference in the sex of the father and daughter would cause the tissue to be rejected by the daughter's immune system.
d. The twins' immune systems would "remember" the same encounters with childhood illnesses.

50. What is the meaning of the underlined word intricacies as it is used in the first sentence of the passage?
a. elaborate interconnections
b. confusion of pathways
c. inherent perplexity
d. comprehensive coverage

ANSWER KEY

1. b.	Lesson 13	
2. d.	Lessons 6, 7, 13	
3. d.	Lesson 1	
4. a.	Lesson 2	
5. c.	Lesson 2	
6. b.	Lesson 18	
7. c.	Lesson 12	
8. b.	Lesson 17	
9. a.	Lesson 1	
10. a.	Lesson 8	
11. d.	Lesson 14	
12. b.	Lesson 8	
13. a.	Lesson 16	
14. d.	Lesson 4	
15. b.	Lesson 13	
16. b.	Lesson 3	
17. c.	Lesson 12	
18. b.	Lesson 13	
19. a.	Lesson 11	
20. d.	Lesson 12	
21. a.	Lesson 8	
22. d.	Lesson 16	
23. d.	Lesson 6	
24. b.	Lesson 11	
25. b.	Lesson 16	

26. d.	Lesson 17
27. a.	Lesson 1
28. a.	Lesson 16
29. c.	Lesson 3
30. b.	Lesson 3
31. c.	Lesson 6
32. d.	Lesson 16
33. d.	Lesson 13
34. c.	Lesson 16
35. c.	Lesson 4
36. a.	Lesson 3
37. b.	Lesson 1
38. d.	Lesson 2
39. a.	Lesson 9
40. c.	Lesson 4
41. a.	Lesson 1
42. b.	Lesson 3
43. c.	Lesson 8
44. b.	Lesson 1
45. c.	Lesson 3
46. d.	Lesson 9
47. a.	Lesson 6
48. b.	Lesson 2
49. b.	Lesson 9
50. a.	Lesson 3

PREPARING FOR A STANDARDIZED TEST

Most of us get nevous about tests, especially standardized tests, where our scores can have a significant impact on our future. Nervousness is natural—and it can even be an advantage if you know how to channel it into positive energy.

The following pages provide suggestions for overcoming test anxiety both in the days and weeks before the test and during the test itself.

TWO TO THREE MONTHS BEFORE THE TEST

The number one best way to combat test anxiety is to **be prepared.** That means two things: Know what to expect on the test and review the material and skills on which you will be tested.

KNOW WHAT TO EXPECT

What knowledge or skills will the exam test? What are you expected to know? What skills will you be expected to demonstrate? What is the format of the test? Multiple choice? True or false? Essay? If possible, go to a bookstore or to the library and get a study guide that shows you what a sample test looks like. Or maybe the agency that's testing you for a job gives out a study guide or conducts study sessions. The fewer surprises you have on test day, the better you will perform. The more you know what to expect, the more confident you will be that you can handle the questions.

REVIEW THE MATERIAL AND SKILLS YOU'LL BE TESTED ON

The fact that you are reading this book means that you've already taken this step in regard to reading comprehension. Now, are there other steps you can take? Are there other subject areas that you need to review? Can you make more improvement in this or other areas? If you are really nervous, or if it has been a long time since you reviewed these subjects and skills, you may want to buy another study guide, sign up for a class in your neighborhood, or work with a tutor.

The more you know about what to expect on test day and the more comfortable you are with the material and skills to be tested, the less anxious you will be and the better you will do on the test itself.

THE DAYS BEFORE THE TEST

REVIEW, DON'T CRAM

If you have been preparing and reviewing in the weeks before the exam, there's no need to cram a few days before the exam. Cramming is likely to confuse you and make you nervous. Instead, schedule a relaxed review of all that you have learned.

PHYSICAL ACTIVITY

Get some exercise in the days preceding the test. You'll send some extra oxygen to your brain and allow your thinking performance to peak on the day you take the test. Moderation is the key here. You don't want to exercise so much that you feel exhausted, but a little physical activity will invigorate your body and brain. Walking is a terrific, low-impact, energy-building form of exercise.

BALANCED DIET

Like your body, your brain needs the proper nutrients to function well. Eat plenty of fruits and vegetables in the days before the test. Foods that are high in lecithin, such as fish and beans, are especially good choices. Lecithin is a protein your brain needs for peak performance. You may even consider a visit to your local pharmacy to buy a bottle of lecithin tablets several weeks before your test.

REST

Get plenty of sleep the nights before you take the test. Don't overdo it, though, or you'll make yourself as groggy as if you were overtired. Go to bed at a reasonable time, early enough to get the number of hours you need to function **effectively**. You'll feel relaxed and rested if you've gotten plenty of sleep in the days before you take the test.

TRIAL RUN

At some point before you take the test, make a trial run to the testing center to see how long it takes you to get there. Rushing raises your emotional energy and lowers your intellectual capacity, so you want to allow plenty of time on test day to get to the testing center. Arriving ten or fifteen minutes early gives you time to relax and get situated.

MOTIVATION

Plan some sort of celebration—with family or friends, or just by yourself—for after the test. Make sure it's something you'll really look forward to and enjoy. If you have something to look forward to after the test is over, you may find it easier to prepare and keep moving during the test.

TEST DAY

It's finally here, the day of the big test. Set your alarm early enough to allow plenty of time to get to the testing center. Eat a good breakfast. Avoid anything that's really high in sugar, such as donuts. A sugar high turns into a sugar low after an hour or so. Cereal and toast, or anything with complex carbohydrates is a good choice. Eat only moderate amounts. You don't want to take a test feeling stuffed! Your body will channel its energy to your digestive system instead of your brain.

Pack a high-energy snack to take with you. You may have a break sometime during the test when you can grab a quick snack. Bananas are great. They have a moderate amount of sugar and plenty of brain nutrients, such as potassium. Most proctors won't allow you to eat a snack while you're testing, but a peppermint shouldn't pose a problem. Peppermints are like smelling salts for your brain. If you lose your concentration or suffer from a momentary mental block, a peppermint can get you back on track. Don't forget the earlier advice about relaxing and taking a few deep breaths.

Leave early enough so you have plenty of time to get to the test center. Allow a few minutes for unexpected traffic. When you arrive, locate the restroom and use it. Few things interfere with concentration as much as a full bladder. Then find your seat and make sure it's comfortable. If it isn't, tell the proctor and ask to change to something you find more suitable.

Now relax and think positively! Before you know it the test will be over, and you'll walk away knowing you've done as well as you can.

COMBATING TEST ANXIETY

Okay—you know what the test will be on. You've reviewed the subjects and practiced the skills on which you will be tested. So why do you still have that sinking feeling in your stomach? Why are your palms sweaty and your hands shaking?

Even the brightest, most well-prepared test takers sometimes suffer bouts of test anxiety. But don't worry; you can overcome it. Below are some specific strategies to help you.

TAKE THE TEST ONE QUESTION AT A TIME

Focus all of your attention on the one question you're answering. Block out any thoughts about questions you've already read or concerns about what's coming next. Concentrate your thinking where it will do the most good—on the question you're answering now.

DEVELOP A POSITIVE ATTITUDE

Keep reminding yourself that you're prepared. In fact, if you've read this book or any other in the LearningExpress Skill Builders series, you're probably better prepared than most others who are taking the test. Remember, it's only a test, and you're going to do your **best**. That's all anyone can ask of you. If that nagging drill sergeant voice inside your head starts sending negative messages, combat them with positive ones of your own. Tell yourself:

- "I'm doing just fine."
- "I've prepared for this test."
- "I know exactly what to do."
- "I know I can get the score I'm shooting for."

You get the idea. Remember to drown out negative messages with positive ones of your own.

IF YOU LOSE YOUR CONCENTRATION

Don't worry about it! It's normal. During a long test it happens to everyone. When your mind is stressed or overexerted, it takes a break whether you want it to or not. It's easy to get your concentration back if you simply acknowledge the fact that you've lost it and take a quick break. You brain needs very little time (seconds, really) to rest.

Put your pencil down and close your eyes. Take a deep breath, hold it for a moment, and let it out slowly. Listen to the sound of your breathing as you repeat this two more times. The few seconds that this takes is really all the time your brain needs to relax and get ready to focus again. This exercise also helps you control your heart rate, so that you can keep anxiety at bay.

Try this technique several times in the days before the test when you feel stressed. The more you practice, the better it will work for you on the day of the test.

IF YOU FREEZE

Don't worry about a question that stumps you even though you're sure you know the answer. Mark it and go on to the next question. You can come back to the "stumper" later. Try to put it out of your mind completely until you come back to it. Just let your subconscious mind chew on the question while your conscious mind focuses on the other items (one at a time—of course). Chances are, the memory block will be gone by the time you return to the question.

If you freeze before you ever begin the test, here's what to do:

1. Do some deep breathing to help yourself relax and focus.
2. Remind yourself that you're prepared.
3. Take a little time to look over the test.
4. Read a few of the questions.
5. Decide which ones are the easiest and start there.

Before long, you'll be "in the groove."

TIME STRATEGIES

One of the most important—and nerve-wracking—elements of a standardized test is time. You'll only be allowed a certain number of minutes for each section, so it is very important that you use your time wisely.

PACE YOURSELF

The most important time strategy is **pacing yourself**. Before you begin, take just a few seconds to survey the test, making note of the number of questions and of the sections that look easier than the rest. Then, make a rough time schedule based on the amount of time available to you. Mark the halfway point on your test and make a note beside that mark of what the time will be when the testing period is half over.

KEEP MOVING

Once you begin the test, **keep moving**. If you work slowly in an attempt to make fewer mistakes, your mind will become bored and begin to wander. You'll end up making far more mistakes if you're not concentrating. Worse, if you take too long to answer questions that stump you, you may end up running out of time before you finish.

So don't stop for difficult questions. Skip them and move on. You can come back to them later if you have time. A question that takes you five seconds to answer counts as much as one that takes you several minutes, so pick up the easy points first. Besides, answering the easier questions first helps to build your confidence and gets you in the testing groove. Who knows? As you go through the test, you may even stumble across some relevant information to help you answer those tough questions.

DON'T RUSH

Keep moving, but **don't rush.** Think of your mind as a seesaw. On one side is your emotional energy. On the other side is your intellectual energy. When your emotional energy is high, your intellectual capacity is low. Remember how difficult it is to reason with someone when you're angry? On the other hand, when your intellectual energy is high, your emotional energy is low. Rushing raises your emotional energy and reduces your intellectual capacity. Remember the last time you were late for work? All that rushing around probably caused you to forget important things—like your lunch. Move quickly to keep your mind from wandering, but don't rush and get yourself flustered.

CHECK YOURSELF

Check yourself at the halfway mark. If you're a little ahead, you know you're on track and may even have a little time left to check your work. If you're a little behind, you have several choices. You can pick up the pace a little, but do this *only* if you can do it comfortably. Remember—**don't rush!** You can also skip around in the remaining portion of the test to pick up as many easy points as possible. This strategy has one drawback, however. If you are marking a bubble-style answer sheet, and you put the right answers in the wrong bubbles—they're wrong. So pay close attention to the question numbers if you decide to do this.

AVOIDING ERRORS

When you take the test, you want to make as few errors as possible in the questions you answer. Here are a few tactics to keep in mind.

CONTROL YOURSELF

Remember that comparison between your mind and a seesaw? Keeping your emotional energy low and your intellectual energy high is the best way to avoid mistakes. If you feel stressed or worried, stop for a few seconds. Acknowledge the feeling (Hmmm! I'm feeling a little pressure here!), take a few deep breaths, and send yourself a few positive messages. This relieves your emotional anxiety and boosts your intellectual capacity.

DIRECTIONS

In many standardized testing situations a proctor reads the instructions aloud. Make certain you understand what is expected. If you don't, **ask.** Listen carefully for instructions about how to answer the questions and make certain you know how much time you have to complete the task. Write the time on your test if you don't already know how long you have to take the test. If you miss this vital information, **ask for it.** You need it to do well on your test.

ANSWERS

This may seem like a silly warning, but it is important. Place your answers in the right blanks or the corresponding ovals on the answer sheet. Right answers in the wrong place earn no points—they may even lose you points. It's a good idea to check every five to ten questions to make sure you're in the right spot. That way you won't need much time to correct your answer sheet if you have made an error.

READING COMPREHENSION PASSAGES

Standardized tests often feature a section designed to test your reading comprehension. The reading sections often contain passages of a paragraph or more. Here are a few tactics for approaching these sections.

This may seem strange, but a few questions can be answered without reading the passage. If the passage is short (four sentences or so), read the questions first. You may be able to answer them by using your common sense. You can check your answers later after you've actually read the passage. If you're unsure, though, *don't guess;* read the passage carefully. If you can't answer any of the questions, you still know what to look for in the passage. This focuses your reading and makes it easier for you to retain important information. Most questions will deal with isolated details in the passage. If you know what to look for ahead of time, it's easier to find the information.

If a reading passage is long and is followed by more than ten questions, it will take some time to read the questions first. Even so, take a few seconds to skim the questions and read a few of the shorter ones. Then, read the passage actively. Mark up the passage. If you find a sentence that seems to state the main idea of the passage, underline it. As you read through the rest of the passage, number the points that support the main idea. Several questions will deal with this information. If it's underlined and numbered, you can locate it easily. Other questions will ask about specific details. **Cir-cle** information that tells who, what, when, or where. The circles will be easy to locate later if you run across a question that asks for specific information. Marking up a passage in this way also heightens your concentration and makes it more likely that you'll remember the information when you answer the questions following the passage.

CHOOSING THE RIGHT ANSWERS BY PROCESS OF ELIMINATION

Make sure you understand what the question is asking. If you're not sure of what's being asked, you'll never know whether you've chosen the right answer. So figure out what the question is asking. If the answer isn't readily apparent, look for clues in the answer choices. Notice the similarities and differences in the answer choices. Sometimes this helps to put the question in a new perspective and makes it easier to answer. If you're still not sure of the answer, use the process of elimination. First, eliminate any answer choices that are obviously wrong. Then reason your way through the remaining choices. You may be able to use relevant information from other parts of the test. If you can't eliminate any of the answer choices, you might be better off to skip the question and come back to it later. If you can't eliminate any answer choices to improve your odds when you come back later, then make a guess and move on.

IF YOU'RE PENALIZED FOR WRONG ANSWERS

You **must know** whether there's a penalty for wrong answers before you begin the test. If you don't, ask the proctor before the test begins. Whether you make a guess or not depends upon the penalty. Some standardized tests are scored in such a way that every wrong answer reduces your score by one fourth or one half of a point. Whatever the penalty, if you can eliminate enough choices to make the odds of answering the question better than the penalty for getting it wrong, make a guess.

Let's imagine you are taking a test in which each answer has four choices and you are penalized one fourth of a point for each wrong answer. If you have no clue and cannot eliminate any of the answer choices, you're better off leaving the question blank because the odds of answering correctly are one in four. This makes the penalty and the odds equal. However, if you can eliminate one of the choices, the odds are now in your favor. You have a one in three chance of answering the question correctly. Fortunately, few tests are scored using such elaborate means, but if your test is one of them, know the penalties and calculate your odds before you take a guess on a question.

IF YOU FINISH EARLY

Use any time you have left at the end of the test or test section to check your work. First, make certain you've put the answers in the right places. As you're doing this, make sure you've answered each question only once. Most standardized tests are scored in such a way that questions with more than one answer are marked wrong. If you've erased an answer, make sure you've done a good job. Check for stray marks on your answer sheet that could distort your score.

After you've checked for these obvious errors, take a second look at the more difficult questions. You've probably heard the folk wisdom about never changing an answer. It's not always good advice. If you have a good reason for thinking a response is wrong, change it.

AFTER THE TEST

Once you've finished, *congratulate yourself*. You've worked hard to prepare; now it's time to enjoy yourself and relax. Remember that celebration you planned before the test? Now it's time to go to it!

GOOD LUCK!

A·P·P·E·N·D·I·X
ADDITIONAL RESOURCES B

eading is like exercise: If you don't keep doing it, you'll get out of shape. Like muscles that grow stronger and bigger with each repetition, your reading skills will grow stronger and stronger with each text that you read. But if you stop working out, your reading comprehension muscles will deteriorate, and you may find yourself struggling with material that you could have easily understood several months ago.

So don't stop now! You've really just begun. Reading comprehension is a skill to build throughout your whole lifetime.

TIPS FOR CONTINUING TO IMPROVE YOUR READING

The following are some ways you can continue to strengthen your reading comprehension skills:

- **Read!** Read anything—books, newspapers, magazines, novels, poems. The more you read, the better. Set yourself a reading goal: one book a month, two books while you're on vacation, a half hour of reading every night before bed. There's a list of suggested books at the end of this section; try some.
- **Discover new authors.** Check out the best-seller list and try one of the books on that list. If it's a best-seller, it's probably a book that appeals to a wide variety of readers, and chances are good that you'll like it.

- Spend time in bookstores and libraries. There are bound to be books and authors out there that appeal to some of your interests. Don't be afraid to ask a salesperson or librarian to help you: Describe your interests and your preferences in style, and he or she can help you find books you'll enjoy reading.
- Join a reading group. Most cities and towns have a club that meets every two weeks or each month to discuss a selected book. In these groups, you'll get to discuss your ideas and questions with a group of friends and associates in an informal setting. If your area doesn't have a reading group, start your own. You and your friends can take turns choosing which book you'll read and discuss.
- Review this book periodically to refresh yourself about the basics. Try some of the Skill Building exercises at the end of each lesson on a regular basis.

SUGGESTED READING LIST

Below is a list of books, organized by subject categories. Choose a category that interests you, and try some of the books listed there.

SCIENCE FICTION

Fahrenheit 451 by Ray Bradbury
The Left Hand of Darkness by Ursula LeGuin
Stranger in a Strange Land by Robert Heinlein
1984 by George Orwell
Jurassic Park by Michael Crighton

SCIENCE/MEDICINE

The Lives of a Cell by Lewis Thomas
Mortal Lessons by Richard Selzer

FANTASY

The Hobbit by J. R. R. Tolkien
On a Pale Horse by Piers Anthony

AUTOBIOGRAPHY

The Autobiography of Malcolm X by Malcolm X
The Story of My Life by Helen Keller
The Diary of Anne Frank by Anne Frank
The Heroic Slave by Frederick Douglas
I Know Why the Caged Bird Sings by Maya Angelou
Having Our Say by Sarah L. and Elizabeth Delaney
Black Boy by Richard Wright
*Everything I Need to Know I Learned in
   Kindergarten* by Robert Fulghum

HISTORICAL/SOCIAL ISSUES

Of Mice and Men by John Steinbeck
The Color Purple by Alice Walker
The Last of the Mohicans
   by James Fenimore Cooper
To Kill a Mockingbird by Harper Lee
The Joy Luck Club by Amy Tan
The Sun Also Rises by Ernest Hemingway
The Lord of the Flies by William Golding
Dangerous Minds by LouAnne Johnson
Schindler's List by Thomas Keneally

WAR

Red Badge of Courage by Stephen Crane
All Quiet on the Western Front
   by Erich Maria Remarque
Hiroshima by John Hershey

COMING OF AGE

A Separate Peace by John Knowles

The Catcher in the Rye by J. D. Salinger

The House on Mango Street by Sandra Cisneros

SHORT STORIES

The short stories of Ernest Hemingway

Love Life by Bobbie Ann Mason

Girls at War by Chinua Achebe

The Stories of Eva Luna by Isabel Allende

INSPIRATIONAL/SPIRITUAL

A Simple Path by Mother Theresa

The Tibetan Book of Living and Dying
        by Sogyal Rinpoche

Care of the Soul by Thomas Moore

Hinds' Feet on High Places by Hannah Hurnard

The Tao of Pooh and *The Te of Piglet*
        by Benjamin Hoff

The Holy Bible

The Koran

Tao Te Ching by Lao Tzu

DETECTIVE/THRILLER

Agatha Christie's murder mysteries

A Time To Kill, The Client by John Grisham

The "A is for . . ." series by Sue Grafton

Novels by Sara Paretsky

Sherlock Holmes stories by Sir Arthur Conan
Doyle

MYTHOLOGY

Mythology by Edith Hamilton

American Indian Myths and Legends by Richard
Erdoes and Alfonso Ortiz